Smuggling in Kent and Sussex
1700–1840

D0167802

Smuggling in Kent and Sussex

1700–1840

MARY WAUGH

COUNTRYSIDE BOOKS
NEWBURY, BERKSHIRE

FIRST PUBLISHED 1985
REPRINTED 1986, 1987, 1994

© Mary Waugh 1985

ISBN 0 905392 48 5

The cover illustration *Beach Landing*
is from a drawing by Edward Dowden

Designed by Mon Mohan
Produced through MRM Associates Ltd., Reading
Typeset in England by Acorn Bookwork, Salisbury, Wiltshire
Printed in England by J. W. Arrowsmith Ltd., Bristol

Contents

Introduction

Behind the church at Patcham, on the edge of Brighton and close to the London road, is a gravestone inscribed 'Daniel Skayles, Aged 34 who was <u>unfortunately</u> shot on Thursday Evening Nov 17th 1796'. The pious verse below this inscription exhorts those who pass to let fall a pitying tear on his behalf. For Daniel Skayles was a smuggler, and one of many killed during the period extending roughly from 1700 to 1840, when large scale smuggling was widespread throughout Britain. Daniel would have called himself a free trader; according to local tradition he was pursued and shot by an Exciseman after he had emerged from one of the secret passageways running between the cellars of houses and inns in Patcham High Street.

The sentiments on his tombstone reflect the common attitudes of his day among all levels of society. It was Adam Smith who maintained that while a smuggler could be blamed for violating the laws of his country, he rarely violated those of natural justice, and would have made an excellent citizen 'had not the laws of his country made that a crime which nature never meant to do so'. In fact the smuggling story is thoroughly discreditable, and especially so in Kent and Sussex during the eighteenth century, when large gangs terrorised the countryside, at times resorting to blackmail, extortion and murder to maintain control. In the long struggle between the free traders and the various preventive services there was hideous violence, needless suffering, villainy and greed, but also determination, skill and courage on both sides. This was a significant episode in our social history. For more than a century the black economy played a major role in everyday life, probably accounting in peak years for a quarter of all of England's overseas trade, and employing up to 40,000 at a time.

Smugglers in Kent and Sussex, nearest to both the London market and the continental suppliers, were leaders in the field. If Excise returns made to the Prime Minister around 1782 are to be believed, a quarter of all the smuggling vessels then operating round the coasts of England and Wales were based there, and a third of all the tea and well over half the gin being fraudulently landed came into these two counties. Inevitably these were also the most heavily protected coasts; at one point almost a quarter of all the Coastguards covering the entire British Isles were concentrated here. In this fraught situation, successful smugglers disguised their activities whenever possible. One of the few whose career is known in some detail is Gabriel Tomkins, who started as a bricklayer in Tunbridge Wells. He then became in turn the leader of a smuggling gang, a Custom House

7

officer and an outlawed highwayman, and ended on the gallows in 1750. The stories which can be pieced together from letters written at the time, and the recorded reminiscences of men who took part, reveal a wealth of unexpected detail. Who today would suspect the battles which once raged on the seafront at Bexhill, along the main streets of Worthing or in sedate London suburbs? It was not simply a question of 'brandy for the parson and baccy for the clerk' but of French prisoners slipping away on board the oyster boats of Whitstable, and seamen from Deal rowing across the Channel swathed in gold guineas to pay Napoleon's troops.

Tangible links with this violent period are relatively few, though there are kegs, grappling hooks, flink pistols and signalling lanterns in certain museum collections. But what have survived are the many authentic smuggling inns, and elegant eighteenth-century mansions, known to have been built from the proceeds of free trading. Most of the hiding places and tunnels have now fallen in or been sealed, but occasionally a bulldozer reveals secrets two centuries old. I am particularly grateful to the householders and innkeepers whose cellars and hiding places I have been able to inspect! At intervals along the coast one can still find the watch houses of the Coast Blockade (forerunners of the Coastguard cottages) where parties of naval seamen kept nightly vigil, from windows set to command a favourite beach. Above all, the countryside in which so many incidents took place can still be readily identified.

The aim of this book has therefore been to set authentic detail from the smuggling epoch alongside the places where these events occurred. For those who may wish to investigate for themselves, there are suggestions on attractive places to visit and walks to try, associated with the smuggling story, and evocative of what took place two centuries ago. As it happens, contraband was landed on virtually every holiday beach from Whitstable round to Selsey Bill and beyond. All manner of struggles took place on the chalk cliffs of Dover and their counterparts along the Seven Sisters coast of Sussex. Almost all the centres which were once gang headquarters are now exceptionally attractive Wealden villages, and there are several castles and many fascinating churches and inns which deserve investigation. The house where George Ransley, leader of the last Kent gang, sold contraband spirit to enthusiastic customers can still be seen, and that at Brookland from which the local doctor was led blindfold to treat smugglers injured in a famous battle on Romney Marsh.

Exploring the smuggling countryside of Kent and Sussex is a form of industrial archaeology, and the revival of interest in what took place here is part of a wider awareness of the fascination of the English landscape. What is more, we are once again a smuggling nation, though the methods, the participants and the contraband have greatly changed.

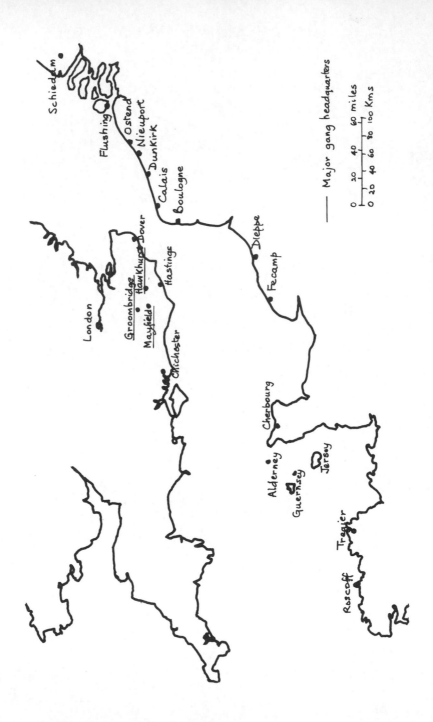

Schiedam

Flushing
Ostend
Nieuport
Dunkirk
Calais
Boulogne

London

Groombridge
Hawkhurst
Mayfield
Hastings
Dover

Chichester

Dieppe
Fecamp

Cherbourg
Alderney
Guernsey
Jersey

Roscoff
Treguier

—— Major gang headquarters

0   20   40   60 miles
0 20 40 60 80 100 Kms

1
The Industry in its Heyday

'The smugglers had reigned a long time uncontrolled; the officers of the Customs were too few to encounter them; they rode in troops to fetch their goods, and carried them off in triumph in daylight; nay, so audacious had they grown, that they were not afraid of the regular troops that were sent into the country to keep them in awe; of which we have several instances. If any of them happened to be taken, and the proof ever so clear against him, no magistrate in the country durst commit him to gaol; if he did he was sure to have his house or barns set on fire, or some other mischief done him, if he was so happy to escape with his life. . . .'

This is how the situation in 1749 was described by 'A Gentleman of Chichester' (in all probability the Duke of Richmond from Good-wood) who was present during the great Chichester Special Assize, at which some of the most notorious smugglers from Kent and Sussex were finally condemned to death. To understand why these conditions of lawlessness and intimidation had come about, we need to look back at the way control over our overseas trade had evolved through the centuries.

The right of the king to raise revenue from duties on goods carried into or out of this country goes back many centuries, and smuggling in one form or another is equally ancient. Over the years the legislation governing the rates of tax became enormously complicated, and the task of collecting the duty was the responsibility of the Custom House officers at the legal quays and recognised ports to which trading was restricted. Then during the Civil War additional revenue was raised by imposing Excise Duty on certain goods manufactured within the country, such as candles and beer. This very unpopular tax on items in daily use was at first intended as a temporary measure, but it was found convenient to retain it and extend its scope. During the eigh-

11

teenth century, therefore, many imported goods were liable to both Customs and Excise duties, and the net effect was often to double or even treble their cost. It was obviously to the advantage of everyone (except the government!) if such items could be brought into the country free of tax. The higher the levels of tax, the greater the incentive to smuggle.

Restrictions on trade in certain items, designed to protect home industry or national security, had the same effect. It had been forbidden to export cannon from the Wealden iron works at the time of the Spanish Armada, for instance, and there were later restrictions on exporting Cornish tin or Cumbrian graphite; inevitably a lively smuggling traffic had grown up in each case. But it was the restrictions on the export of English wool which had the greatest impact. In an attempt to protect our cloth industry, it was made illegal to export wool from other than designated ports, and for some years after 1662 this was a capital offence. The embargo was particularly irksome to wool producers on the downs and coastal marshes of south east England, and led predictably to widespread flouting of the restrictions. Around 1700 it is thought that 150,000 packs of wool a year were being shipped out illegally from Kent and Sussex, within days of a shearing.

The owling trade, as it came to be known, was often controlled by Huguenot families who had come to England as refugees from religious persecution, and who retained close links with their relatives across the Channel. The continental clothiers conspired with the English wool producers to ensure that the trade continued, and cargoes of lace and brandy were shipped back in part payment for the prized high quality wool. In 1713 two Frenchmen were caught in a typical incident at Fairlight near Hastings, while trying to negotiate a deal of this type. Moreover, foreign vessels, known as 'coopers', regularly lay for days off our south and east coasts, and even within the Tyne and Humber estuaries, acting as floating supermarkets, much as today's cross-Channel ferries tempt the customer with 'duty free' bargains.

The owling trade brought into being the first important smuggling gang, which was based at Mayfield in the Sussex Weald before 1720, and the farmers, shopkeepers and others involved built up the capital and business contacts from which the later import smuggling developed. Illegal shipments of wool and even live sheep continued through the eighteenth century, but after about 1720 the whole emphasis of the smuggling trade shifted to the bringing in of tea, spirits, tobacco and luxury items.

Several other factors contributed to the rapid expansion of smuggling after 1720, and to the degree of support for the trade at all levels of

12

society. For one thing the economy of Kent and Sussex was in a depressed state. The sharp decline of the iron smelting and cloth making industries of the Weald had reduced many to acute poverty. A farm labourer could earn no more than 7/- or 8/- for a full week's work, and was likely to be unemployed for part of the winter, whereas for a successful night's effort carrying contraband he could expect about 10/- if everything went well. The citizens of the towns along the coast were also in difficulties. Before the Norman Conquest the five prosperous ports of Sandwich, Dover, Hythe, Romney and Hastings and the two 'ancient towns' of Rye and Winchelsea had joined together to form the Cinque Ports Confederation. In return for providing the medieval kings with men and ships to form a navy, they had won important rights of self government and immunity from the earliest form of Customs duty, a concession which their citizens intended to retain long after their contribution to the navy had ceased!

By 1700 both the head ports and the lesser members of the confederation, known as limbs, had fallen on hard times. The sea, on which their earlier prosperity depended, now filled their harbours with shingle or washed away protecting headlands. During the sixteenth century the seamen of Winchelsea had turned to piracy to replace the wine trade which had once brought them wealth. Smuggling offered even better prospects throughout the eighteenth century, and men from all the Cinque Ports were to be actively involved.

It was not just in Kent and Sussex that the mass of people lived in poverty. Eighteenth century society was rigidly stratified; the labouring poor had little opportunity to improve their lot, or even to move out of the parish of their birth. Smuggling, like poaching, was to some extent a form of social protest against the harshness and drabness of this existence. At the other end of the social scale, most of the landed gentry grew richer as the century progressed. Public appointments were frequently filled through patronage, and corruption was rife. Sir Robert Walpole, as Whig Prime Minister from 1721 to 1742, built up his private fortune while at the same time working hard to introduce order into the collection of revenue.

In Sussex three major figures stood out against the prevailing lawlessness. Thomas Pelham-Holles, Duke of Newcastle (who had Sussex estates at Bishopstone and Laughton) and his brother Henry Pelham at Stanmer House, Brighton held important political office for over forty years between them, and at Goodwood House the Duke of Richmond was implacable in his campaign against smuggling.

There were other reasons for widespread public disaffection. In 1714, following Queen Anne's death, England accepted Hanoverian George I as king, but there were many who regarded the exiled James Stuart as the legal claimant to the throne. Disaffection among Jaco-

Smugglers, a print of 1799 engraved by J P Smith, which shows the typical features of a small landing. Reproduced by kind permission of Alan Hay.

bite supporters smouldered on, to surface in the unsuccessful rising in support of the Old Pretender in 1715. There is abundant evidence of links between Jacobite sympathisers and the smugglers. The Mayfield gang are said to have drunk King James' health in 1715; in 1721 an extraordinary conspiracy was hatched which aimed to seize King George, the Tower and the Bank of England. The participants included a Sussex baronet called Goring, and a smuggling gang known as the Waltham Blacks (the leaders were later banished). In 1744, when Bonnie Prince Charlie and troops under Marshal Saxe were in Dunkirk and poised to invade England, three Jacobite sympathisers from West Sussex were among those who tried to join the prince in France. (In the event the three were betrayed when they sought the help of the smugglers at Hooe near Pevensey, in their attempt to cross the Channel.) When the next year Bonnie Prince Charlie won support in Scotland and led his followers as far as Derby on the road to London, the government prudently sent several army units to the known smuggling strongholds in Kent and Sussex. Jacobite hopes were to be finally extinguished by defeat at Culloden in 1746.

At all times the main factor behind the huge expansion of smuggling was the high level of import duties, brought about by the need to raise revenue to fight a succession of wars. The conflicts of the early eighteenth century had only limited impact on our trade, but a damaging struggle began in 1739, and warfare continued during 44 of the following 75 years. All these struggles involved war at sea, and France was our enemy on most occasions. As a result, not only were heavy duties imposed on trade, but French privateers regularly attacked shipping along the Channel coast.

The first climax of smuggling activity came during the 1740s, when the country was beset by Jacobite disaffection within, and the War of the Austrian Succession overseas. It seems likely that up to a quarter of our overseas trade was being smuggled at this time, though no statistics exist. With the return of peace in 1748, some reductions in duty, and the series of trials which broke up the Kent and Sussex gangs, there was a lull in operations for some years. Then came the Seven Years War, fought in four continents, and the even more damaging War of American Independence. Duties had once again climbed to ridiculous heights. The country was denuded of the manpower needed to control widespread lawlessness, and smuggling reached a second peak around 1780. It was then rapidly reduced by the intervention of William Pitt, who cut the duty on tea from 129% to 12½% in 1784 (and increased Window Tax to make good the resulting deficit).

The French Revolutionary Wars and the Napoleonic Wars which

lasted (with one brief intermission) from 1793 to 1815, led to certain new forms of smuggling. French aristocrats were helped to flee to England during the terrible days after the French Revolution. Another item smuggled out of France at this time was part of the Duke of Orleans' collection of pictures, shipped into this country as wine by Sir Thomas Moore Slade, using his authority as Agent-Victualler at Chatham Dockyard. The seamen of Deal and Folkestone specialised in running gold guineas to France, where the currency had collapsed and the money was needed to pay Napoleon's troops. It is known that City bankers were behind this lucrative speculation, when a guinea worth 21/- in England could fetch 30/- in Paris. Meanwhile the numerous French prisoners, often held in terrible conditions on prison hulks in the Thames estuary, were helped to escape by Kent oyster fishermen. Many smugglers found lucrative employment as spies or double agents, and some became naval pilots.

A third and short-lived peak of smuggling began with the return home of some 250,000 soldiers and seamen after the victory at Waterloo. Many had difficulty finding alternative employment, though the early stages of the Industrial Revolution were creating new oppor-

Unlading a cutter, a print engraved by B T Pouncy in 1785, which shows the long bowsprit of the vessel and other aspects of a landing.

tunities in the Midlands and North, and the first fashionable coastal resorts were developing. In rural Kent and Sussex poverty and unemployment continued, and were to lead to riots and emigration during the 1830s. What finally eliminated organised smuggling was the establishment of an effective preventive service, combined with the change to free trade policies after 1840.

As the level of smuggling activity fluctuated over the years from 1700 to 1840, so too did the profitability of particular items. The smugglers were opportunists, prepared to handle a wide range of goods. Luxury items, such as fine wines, silk, lace, fashionable clothes, glass and china were often brought in to order (as an invoice found among goods seized at Newhaven in 1822 was to show). Among the more prosaic items sometimes carried were salt and paper. Tea, spirits and tobacco were the staples of the trade, but spices, coffee, chocolate, playing cards, jewellery and even human hair appear among the many items seized.

For most of the eighteenth century the best returns came from smuggled tea. This was cheap to buy and easy to handle (it came suitably packaged in oilskin bags). Around 1740 the cheapest grades of tea could be bought in Holland for 6d a pound, and sold in England for 3/- or 4/- a pound, compared with the lowest legal cost of 5/-. Not surprisingly England was then drinking more than three times as much smuggled tea as that legally imported. In a bid to stop this rampant law breaking, the government cut the duty on tea dramatically in 1745. It is one of the ironies of the smuggling story that when the Hawkhurst gang rescued their tea from Poole Custom House in 1746, in a venture for which a number paid with their lives, their profit margin on the cargo had been drastically reduced. Higher duties were soon reimposed, however, and by 1780 the legitimate dealers (including a certain Richard Twining) lobbied the government for protection against unfair competition and the practice of adulterating tea with hedgerow leaves. William Pitt then destroyed the profitability of tea smuggling by removing most of the duty in 1784. However, in the three years immediately before this reform, Excise officers estimated that over 2,550,000 lbs of tea had been fraudulently landed on the coasts of Kent and Sussex, or one third of all the tea smuggled into the whole of England and Wales.

Tobacco smuggling replaced the illegal tea trade after 1800, and this was particularly profitable around 1820, when the duty stood at 4/- a pound. At one point it was estimated that tobacco costing £100 in Flushing was worth ten times as much in England. The duty on tobacco remained high throughout the nineteenth century, as indeed it still is, and it is interesting to find a court case in 1983 involving the smuggling of tobacco from Belgium into the Leeds area! Much of the tobacco was brought into the main ports by documentation frauds rather than run on open beaches. Most came in leaf form or as stalks (for snuff), and was either manufactured illegally or infiltrated into the legal trade. Supplies came from America, either directly or via Ireland, so it was the west coast and the Bristol Channel ports which played most part in this trade.

French brandy was always a favourite item of contraband. Its import was forbidden during the years of war with France, and at other times it carried a duty of £1 per gallon. Gin (or Geneva) originated in Holland, and had become popular in England during the reign of William and Mary. It carried no duty to begin with, and this led to the epidemic of drunkenness we know best through the drawings of Hogarth. After 1736 gin too paid duty at £1 per gallon, and it was soon to become the most popular item of contraband on the coasts of England nearest to Holland. Rum from the West Indies was also smuggled, but much less frequently. The spirits came packaged for handling (and sinking when necessary) in small kegs known as tubs. A tub normally held one half anker, or between 3½ and 4 gallons, and to increase its value further, the spirit was usually 70° over proof. It had therefore to be 'let down' after landing, by the addition of water and caramel colouring, an operation which could create problems. It also meant that enthusiasts for the raw spirit sometimes died of alcoholic poisoning after a cask was broached. More gin than brandy was brought in on the south east coast because of its proximity to Holland. According to estimates made by Excise officers around 1780, well over half of all the contraband gin brought ashore in England and Wales was being landed in Kent and Sussex, a grand total of 1,808,000 gallons in three years. By contrast 552,000 gallons of brandy were run here over the same period, a merely 14% of the national total.

Although smuggling was more important on the Kent and Sussex coasts than anywhere else in the country, virtually every accessible beach from west Cornwall to north Scotland was used at one time or another. The shores of Essex and East Anglia, the bays near Whitby in North Yorkshire, the lonely sands of Northumberland and the Scottish harbours near Montrose were favourites along the east coast. Danish and Scandinavian seamen took part in the trade, and the scale of smuggling led to the growth of supply industries on the continent. France and Holland imported tea almost solely to support the smugglers. Tobacco factories were set up at Flushing and Nieuport, and distilleries at Schiedam and Dunkirk to the same end. When it became illegal to build the specialised vessels or make the ropes and casks used for the trade in England, those industries also crossed the Channel.

The shores of Poole Harbour and Christchurch Bay were particularly important further west, and smuggling in Devon and Cornwall was to continue long after it had been brought under control further east. One reason for extensive smuggling along our western coasts was the existence of islands outside Customs control, which could act as depots for the trade. The Channel Isles, and especially Guernsey, flourished as supply bases until effective Customs control was established in 1805. Thereafter the merchants and manufacturers of specialised containers moved operations to Cherbourg, Roscoff and the Brittany coast. The economy of the Scilly Isles declined disastrously once Customs control was extended there in 1828, and for a time Lundy and other small islands in the Bristol Channel became bases for the trade. The Isle of Man acted as depot for contraband shipped into North Wales, the Wirral and the Solway coasts until 1765, when the full duties were imposed; thereafter Ireland became the chief base for operations, and remained the main source of contraband tobacco until after 1850.

A Footnote from France.

Michel Caron, writing from Calais, has given unexpected information on one form of industrial espionage during the Napoleonic Wars. Newly developed lace making machines built in Nottingham were smuggled out in parts for reassembly in France around 1816 or 1817. This trade, and the export of English cotton yarns were, of course, prohibited. As there appears to be no record of such illegal exports in our Custom House accounts, it seems probable that the trade went undetected, and English lace makers settled profitably in Calais. The story reverses the more usual one of "laces for a lady" smuggled *into* Britain.

2
Smugglers and
Preventivemen

Dr Johnson defined a smuggler as a wretch who, in defiance of justice and the laws, imports or exports goods without payment of the customs. John Wesley, another contemporary of the great period of free trading, extended his condemnation to include those who bought or sold smuggled goods, a definition which would have included whole communities. Other definitions were laid down in the various Acts designed to stamp out the trade. For example in 1721, any person who carried firearms or wore a vizard or mask when handling contraband was treated as a smuggler. Of the thousands who took part in the trade, most did so on a casual or part-time basis; only a much smaller number were full-time professionals. There was also the important distinction between the sea smugglers who brought the goods from continental suppliers, and the land gangs responsible for landing and transporting the contraband. When Admiral Vernon sent the following report to the Admiralty in 1745, he was describing the sea smugglers of Kent, and he could have added the seamen from Rye, Hastings and Shoreham to his list. (The extract is from the Parry Collection, by courtesy of HM Customs & Excise.)

.... 'there are said to be in the town of Deal, not less than two hundred able young men and sea-faring people, who are known to have no visible way of getting a living, but by the infamous trade of smuggling, many keeping a horse and arms to be ready at all calls. At Dover it is conjectured there may be four hundred; at Ramsgate and Folkstone three hundred each; and it is said, that within these three weeks no less than nine cutters at a time have gone off from Folkstone to Boulogne; and ... that from the town of Folkstone only a thousand pounds a week is run over to Boulogne in a smuggling way...

This smuggling has converted those employed in it, first from honest industrious fishermen, to lazy, drunken and profligate smugglers, and now to dangerous spies on all our proceedings. ... I can't but think it is a national reproach upon us, to have let their villainy and treachery run to such an extensive length....'

Despite Admiral Vernon's strictures, these men were generally recognised as superb seamen. They had to contend with all the normal hazards of sailing in darkness and at the worst times of year, to keep an appointment on some secluded beach, and in addition to avoid any patrolling preventive vessel. At least during the early eighteenth century, disaster was more likely to arise from shipwreck than from intervention by the small number of revenue craft. One Essex smuggling vessel is said to have made 35 consecutive successful voyages! Later, during the long years of war with France, the ever present danger was capture by an enemy privateer and (like all seamen) the crew had to evade the dreaded press gang.

Virtually every type of craft was used for smuggling at one time or another; naval vessels, revenue cutters, packet boats and pilot boats, even a royal yacht made the occasional venture. However, two types of vessel were increasingly used, and were often specially built for the trade. The large smuggling vessels were luggers, generally from 50 to 200 tons. Some were carvel-built (with timbers edge to edge) for

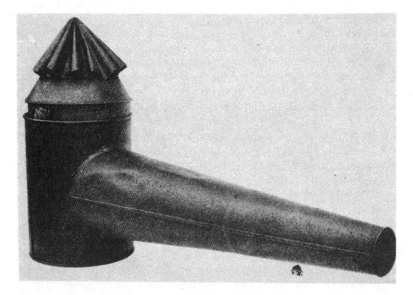

A spout lantern. Made by local craftsmen, these lanterns enabled the smuggler to direct a beam of light at the incoming vessel by uncovering the opening briefly.

greater speed. They normally carried square sails on three masts, and it was the development of fore and aft rigging during the seventeenth century which had given such vessels greater manoeuvrability. Their decks were sometimes protected by a form of breast-work, behind which were mounted carriage and swivel guns. With a crew of perhaps 50, the larger ships were formidable indeed. Both smugglers and revenuemen came increasingly to use cutters (an improved version of the sloops common around 1700). A cutter derived her strength from being clinker or clinch-built (with overlapping timbers). Her tall mast carried a very great spread of canvas, thanks partly to a long bowsprit (which could be brought inboard). Specially built smuggling craft were sometimes built of fir rather than oak, for cheapness as well as speed, since their life expectancy was short!

Many of the larger smuggling vessels were built at Hastings, until the government forced the industry to move to France and the Low Countries. By the 1780s these larger craft were powerful enough to engage naval ships, and sometimes tried to run down and sink their smaller adversaries. They also carried tub boats used to run barrels of spirit ashore. These open rowing boats had a rail on their outer edge along which a necklace of tubs could be hung, ready for instant sinking if danger threatened. Without sinking stones the tubs would float, so various methods of 'sowing a crop' (sinking the casks below the surface at marked spots) were soon developed.

By the 1790s Deal specialised in building long slender galleys rowed by up to 20 men, but having a small sail in addition. These light and cheaply-built boats were particularly used by the guinea smugglers during the Napoleonic Wars. Various smaller, but similar open boats were also used to bring back tubs of spirit left in mid Channel. A galley could be rowed back from Dunkirk to Deal in as little as five hours if the tide was favourable. At Rye the boatbuilders were particularly adept at devising secret compartments to outwit customs officers rummaging a cargo. Another ploy was for the smuggling vessel to claim bogus foreign nationality, and to carry appropriate flags and ship's papers. Admiral Vernon was right to suspect that some acted as spies, and other men were probably double agents. The seamen of Deal were particularly notorious; their actions roused the fury of Prime Minister William Pitt, and in 1784 he retaliated by burning all their vessels as these lay drawn up off the beach to escape the winter storms. Napoleon is said to have received English newspapers by courtesy of a Bexhill smuggler, and Sir John Moore, who was responsible for defending the most vulnerable stretch of coast against an expected invasion, reported 'There is hardly a family in Folkestone which has not relatives settled in Flushing, and there is constant intercourse.' However, most of these seamen remained loyal   23 to Britain; smugglers brought regular reports from France to Welling-ton, and Nelson employed Deal smugglers as pilots because of their skill and experience.

Once the sea smugglers had brought the contraband to the shore, the various land-based groups took over. Lookout men would exchange signals with the vessel, and if danger threatened would warn the ship to withdraw by flashing a light from a special lantern or a flink pistol, or even lighting a clifftop fire (all actions which were punishable offences). The landing party remained concealed until the crucial moment; sometimes several hundred men and horses had been assembled. Most of these men were local labourers hoping to receive more for a single night's work than they could otherwise earn in a week. Those detailed to unload the cargo were protected by others armed at the very least with bats (wooden staves), and often with hangers (swords), cutlasses or firearms. Sometimes a smuggling vessel was beached for unloading; more often small boats were used to carry the goods ashore, and tubs of spirit were pulled in attached to a long rope. A good team could run 500 tubs ashore in 20 minutes. Landings usually took place on nights away from full moon, but on Romney Marsh in 1734 no such precautions were taken. The Secret-ary to the Commissioners of Excise reported that ... 'the smugglers pass and repass to and from the sea-side, forty and fifty in a gang in the day time loaded with teas, brandy and dry goods; that above two hundred mounted smugglers were seen one night upon the sea beach waiting for the loading of six boats and above one hundred were seen to go off loaded with goods; that they march in a body from the beach about four miles into the country and then separate into small par-ties...'

The individual smuggler protected his anonymity with various disguises, such as covering his face or wearing a shepherd's smock, and called his companions and the landing places by nick-names, but the large armed convoys relied on their superior strength to defy all opposition. Whereas West Country smugglers seem generally to have operated in small groups, in Kent and Sussex large and powerful gangs dominated the trade, though innumerable smaller groups also took part. The gang based on the Wealden village of Hawkhurst during the 1740s became the most notorious. Others had developed some years earlier at Mayfield and Groombridge not far away, and we know the names and nicknames of a number of the leading members. Behind such men lay the shadowy figures who provided the capital for ventures which could involve an outlay of £10,000 or more.

Around 1780 the War of American Independence had denuded the country of its armed forces, and for a time smuggling gangs rode defiantly through major towns all over England. A further attempt to

Smugglers Attacked. A popular early 19th century print by an unknown artist. Reproduced by kind permission of Alan Hay.

establish powerful gangs began around 1820. At this time George Ransley led the last important gang in Kent. He had his own foreign suppliers, and retained both a group of seamen and local labourers to act as tub carriers. He used his son as secretary and accountant, and employed his own surgeon and firm of solicitors!

The logistics of a major smuggling run, such as the Hawkhurst gang could have undertaken around 1740, required elaborate organ-

25

Officer—Light Dragoons 1791

An Officer of the Dragoons. These mounted regular soldiers were often called to assist in the prevention of smuggling.

isation. One problem must have been to raise and transport the necessary money, at a time when there was no bank even in Hastings. Sending messages when so many were illiterate, and synchronising the arrival of ship and landing party (with alternative arrangements if the run was foiled) must have taxed their ingenuity. We know they employed various pre-arranged signals, such as the set of windmill sails or animals tethered in particular patterns. If the sea smugglers were excellent sailors, the inland gangs acquired remarkable and widespread knowledge of alternative routes through the countryside.

26

Though they later made use of carts and coaches, most eighteenth century contraband was carried on horseback. It was estimated that a packhorse could carry 280 lbs (127 kg), while a horse and cart could transport five times as much. The horses were often 'borrowed' from local farmers who dared not refuse to cooperate. Incidentally one of the accusations levelled against the smugglers in 1746 was that they had brought in with a cargo of silk a disease affecting horses, which one army captain described as 'general leprosie'.

As head of the preventive services and Mayor of Hastings, John Collier faced equivalent difficulties. He wrote of the awful road conditions, and of flood water reaching up to his saddlebags as he rode through Robertsbridge. He found it best to send goods to London with the regular sailing cutter, skippered by Nicholas Bossum (whom he suspected of smuggling). In 1745 the 'fast' coach which left Hastings at 4 a.m. took three days to reach London, and when ten years later John Collier decided to take the waters at Bath, rather than use the local road, he timed the start of his journey to coincide with low tide, so that his coach could travel west over the firm sands of Pevensey Bay.

Smuggling was very much a high risk occupation. Although some individuals managed to operate through a lifetime, the larger gangs seldom lasted ten years. At times two gangs might work together, but a characteristic of the Hawkhurst men was the way they took over other groups and browbeat them into cooperation. The more successful of the full-time smugglers made their fortunes rapidly, investing part of the money in fine houses with appropriate storage facilities, but the richest rewards went to their financial backers. It is known that London bankers and leading City merchants derived huge profits from smuggling, as they also did from the Slave Trade.

Ranged against both land and sea smugglers were men in the various preventive services, and at the core of this defence were the Custom House officers responsible for legal trade. The Collector was the most senior official at each port, and it is his correspondence with the Board of Customs in London which provides authentic detail on the extent of smuggling. He was also responsible for the warehouse where seizures of contraband were held, often all too insecurely. At important ports like Dover he was assisted by a number of other officers, ranging from his deputy, the Comptroller, down to humble boatmen. (An indication of the numbers involved comes from a report of 1822, when the establishment was 62 at Dover, 28 at Rye and 19 each at Deal and Shoreham.) While the Collector's Clerk battled with a flood of official forms (some still in Latin), the officers most likely to come into direct conflict with the smugglers were the landwaiters, responsible for imported goods, the tide surveyors who rummaged

27

A Smuggler and *The Preventive Service*, by William Heath, prints which illustrate the clothes of the smuggler and the uniform and equipment of a Coastguard in the 1830s.

vessels, and the tidesmen who were put on board a vessel until unloading was completed.

Excisemen constituted a separate, and sometimes rival preventive service. Their original task had been to collect tax on items manufactured in the country, but as Excise duty was later extended to various imported goods, they too had the right to search ships and seize contraband. Both Customs and Excise officers were entitled to call on the help of dragoons (the mounted soldiers), but such assistance often proved totally inadequate. Each group was poorly paid, and their

main incentive for tangling with the smugglers was the chance of reward for a successful seizure. There was also every motive for competition rather than concerted action between them, and this unhappy situation was compounded by the slowness and meanness with which any reward was granted.

To meet the special problem of controlling the illegal export of wool, Riding Officers were appointed and stationed on the most vulnerable stretches of coast. By 1700 there were 300 of these men operating in 19 English countries. Each officer was responsible for providing his own horse, and for night-time patrols along a stretch of coast (4 miles in the worst areas and about 10 miles elsewhere). His job entailed listening to rumours, while keeping his own movements secret and unpredictable, and writing a daily record. He was paid £25 a year, with an allowance for his horse. He could also call on the help of locally-based dragoons, but the number available was small and the men disliked the work. The first Surveyor-General of Riding Officers in Kent was Captain Henry Baker, and from 1735 to 1750 this post was held by John Collier, a lawyer and five times Mayor of Hastings. Among the 2000 letters which have survived from Collier's correspondence (otherwise known as the Sayer Manuscripts) are the best accounts of smuggling in Kent and Sussex at this time. Unfortunately Major Battine, who held the equivalent post in Sussex, left few records.

Conscientious Riding Officers ran a considerable risk of being killed or injured by the smugglers among whom they lived. Some became too old or infirm to discharge their duties, and it is hardly surprising that others succumbed to a mixture of threats and bribery. For example, John Sowton, a West Sussex smuggler, said of the Riding Officer at Lancing in the 1740s 'Damn him, its as easy as can be to make him quiet, for do but dash a bottle of brandy in his face and he is as blind as a beetle.'

The Board of Customs also controlled a small number of vessels which patrolled offshore. By 1700 there were some twenty Revenue craft responsible for the whole coastline, and four of the smaller naval vessels were added specifically to help against the owling trade. More ships were presently made available, and larger, better armed and faster vessels were to form the most significant defence against smuggling by the 1780s. However, even these were seldom a match for the bigger smuggling cutters or the French privateers.

As the smuggling trade increased after 1720, the government responded partly by making more soldiers available to meet particular crises, but chiefly by enacting a flood of legislation, much of which proved difficult to enforce in the absence of adequate manpower and finance. Legislation was aimed first to make smuggling as difficult as possible, and then to catch and punish the offenders. The sequence begins with the Act of 1698 to stop the illegal export of wool. This was followed by a series of Hovering Acts intended to prevent vessels loitering-with-intent outside territorial waters, and at one stage persons loitering within five miles of the coast were also suspect. Vessels below a certain size, and carrying suspect cargo were liable to forefeiture. After 1721 any rowing boat with more than four oars was liable to be seized and destroyed, and there were later measures to forbid the carrying of spirits and tobacco in small containers. The reasoning behind these measures was sensible enough; the problem once again was enforcement. Some successes could be claimed, however. Between 1723 and 1736, 229 smuggling boats had been confiscated, 2000 persons prosecuted, and nearly 200,000 gallons of brandy seized. At the same time 250 Revenue Officers had been beaten or wounded, and six had been murdered.

As the violence escalated, the penalties became increasingly savage. For an unarmed man caught carrying contraband, the penalty in 1700 would have been imprisonment; after 1736 it became transportation, and after 1746 death. By then, an armed smuggler injuring an officer faced being gibbeted, that is, the hanging of his body in chains as a warning to others (a prospect which horrified the toughest villain). But the measures which had the greatest impact and which drove the gangs to terrorise whole communities and torture suspected informers were the Smuggling Acts of 1736 and 1746. Under the former, any smuggler, even if in gaol, could have a free pardon if he confessed all and gave the names of his associates. In 1746 the names of known smugglers were published in the London Gazette. If thereafter a gazetted man did not surrender within 40 days, he was automatically sentenced to death, and anyone turning in such a man was entitled to a reward of £500. This is the Act against which to set the savage and bestial actions of the Kent and Sussex gangs. The climax came in 1749 and 1750 when the Hawkhurst and Groombridge gangs were finally broken up. The Duke of Richmond, who had conducted a personal campaign against these villains, was able to report that in two years 35 smugglers had been executed, 8 had died in gaol, one had drowned and another been pardoned.

Though violence and bloodshed continued as late as the 1830s, it was never again on the same scale. The full severities of the Smuggling Act of 1746 had been introduced for an experimental period of seven years, and later legislation softened its provisions. By 1782, when Britain had been brought low by the War of American Independence, an Act of Oblivion was proclaimed. This allowed any smuggler who could find one landsman and one seaman to serve the country, to commute a penalty up to £500. And for two landsmen and two seamen he could go free of any penalty, however great! But the net was tightening around the smuggling fraternity, and a scale of rewards for their capture presently evolved. In mercenary fashion, a smuggler who defected to the Revenue service was known as a ten shilling man (since this was his weekly pay), while one handed over to the authorities earned his captor £20.

Meanwhile the struggle against the sea smugglers assumed greater importance. Both the Customs and the Excise now maintained patrol vessels, and private individuals were encouraged to build and sail ships under contract to the Board of Customs. The incentive, once again, was prize money, and William Arnold, Collector of Customs at Cowes and father of the famous school headmaster, was one who took up this challenge. By 1784 the number of Revenue cruisers had risen to 44, crewed by over a thousand men, the largest ship being about 200 tons. Naval vessels played an increasing role against the smugglers, and by 1786 naval officers had powers to arrest and search suspect craft. By this time men in the Revenue service could claim immunity from the press gangs, and a scale of compensation for injury had been worked out. (£10 was paid for the loss of a hand or foot!) During the long wars with France some Revenue vessels were withdrawn to do battle against French privateers; not to be outdone, the captains of large smuggling ships took out Letters of Marque and became privateers in their turn!

The fight against smuggling gained ground slowly after 1800, as measures intended to thwart Napoleon destroyed the privacy of many favourite landing places. Barracks, signal stations and Martello Towers lined the Kent and Sussex coasts, and with the completion of the Royal Military Canal in 1806, the smuggling beaches of Romney Marsh were effectively cut off from their hinterland. In 1809 the Preventive Waterguard was established. Thereafter boat crews, under the command of a Boatsitter, rowed nightly patrols along each stretch of coast, and the first Watch Houses were built to accommodate these men, recruited from outside the area to avoid collusion with local smugglers. The Riding Officers were still retained as a Landguard; indeed in Kent and Sussex their patrols continued until after 1850.

The real change came after the defeat of Napoleon at Waterloo, and the return home of some 250,000 soldiers and sailors. Many turned to smuggling in the absence of alternative employment, but in 1816 Captain McCulloch put to his masters at the Admiralty proposals for establishing a Coast Blockade. This scheme was initially tried out along the Kent coast between the North and South Forelands, under the control of McCulloch from HMS *Ganymede* at Deal. It was soon extended to all the coasts from Sheerness round to Beachy Head. By 1824 a total of 2784 men were employed in making nightly patrols, and the Coast Blockade was further extended to Chichester. Groups of naval seamen under a naval lieutenant were based either in Martello Towers or in Watch Houses built at intervals of two or three miles along the vulnerable coasts. The seamen disliked their task and were frequently offered bribes to allow goods to be run. Several fell to their deaths from the cliffs and others were killed or injured in fights with the smugglers. Among the more positive aspects of the system were early attempts to rescue people by life-saving apparatus. Another rescue in 1824 concerned a cargo of apples brought ashore from a wreck near Beachy Head, and later sold in Newhaven!

Meanwhile a national Coast Guard had been established in 1821 to patrol the coasts not protected by the Coast Blockade, and in 1831

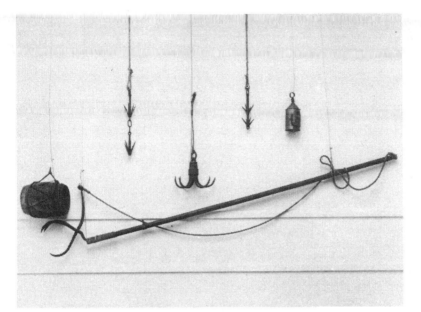

Equipment used by smugglers, including several types of grapnel for creeping up tubs from the sea or shallow ponds, and the typical small keg or tub of spirits.

this service took over from the Blockade in Kent and Sussex when the latter was disbanded. Experience had now shown the most effective means of control. Some Coastguards served in Revenue cutters at sea, and others manned a rowing guard offshore, but most were shore-based parties patrolling a regular beat along the coast. The men were encouraged to seize the smugglers rather than the contraband. From the beginning the service was under naval command, though responsible to the Board of Customs, and it eventually became in effect a naval reserve. Recruits were based away from their home area, and the familiar Coastguard cottages were built as a result. The Coastguard had become a uniformed and disciplined force, and as smuggling declined, the service became increasingly involved in rescue and livesaving work.

After 1820 the smugglers had to resort to bribery and every sort of deception to land their goods. Tubs of spirit were sunk offshore, to be grappled up later with oysters and crab pots. In the cat-and-mouse tactics which developed, tubs were towed in under the keel of a boat, in a canvas tube behind it, or in carefully contrived rafts. They were

33

camouflaged or hidden under other cargo, and fishing boats, packet boats and colliers were employed. Official reports from this period contain drawings of ingenious methods of concealment; boats had false bottoms and hidden compartments, hollow masts and even hollow oars. Rummaging a vessel came to involve very careful inspection and measurement, and dexterous use of a gimlet! Many of the tunnels and secret passages probably date from this period. One particularly discreditable episode involved the Tide Surveyor's boat at Deal. The six-man crew regularly used this to bring tubs ashore, and when they were caught doing so in July 1825, close to the Watch House, the consequences included demotion for the Collector at Deal.

The final blow came when the reduction of Customs and Excise duties made most smuggling unprofitable. As an official report of 1839 put it, 'smuggling as a well-organised system no longer exists'. Nevertheless it was thought prudent to retain a total of 1451 Coastguards along the Kent and Sussex shores during the 1840s.

The London Market and its Main Suppliers

Once the contraband had been successfully landed, its speedy marketing was essential. The small family business probably served no more than a local market, but big profits required major investment, large scale organisation and contacts with the London merchants who alone could handle tea by the ton or consignments of spirit worth over £1000. Accordingly, much of the contraband landed not just in Kent and Sussex, but also in Suffolk, Essex, Hampshire and Dorset was destined for the London markets. The immediate objective was to mix the uncustomed goods with their legally imported counterpart; once that was achieved, there was little further danger of detection. This infiltration of contraband took place in market towns like Canterbury and Faversham in Kent, or Hailsham, Lewes and Horsham in Sussex, but most of the largest smuggling convoys headed straight for London.

In 1700 London had only recently recovered from the twin disasters of the Fire and the Plague. There were probably 675,000 residents, nearly all of whom lived north of the Thames. South of the river the only built up area was in Southwark close to London Bridge, which was still the only bridge. Smugglers approaching from the south passed through small hamlets set in fields and commons, which were still the haunts of highwaymen. Their main south London depot was the hamlet of Stockwell, about 3½ miles from the City and between the commons of Clapham and Kennington. It was conveniently near the horseferry across the Thames at Lambeth, though Lambeth itself was no more than a single street of houses at this time. House building did not begin in this part of south London until after the opening of Westminster Bridge in 1750, and Blackfriars Bridge in 1769. Stockwell was still an isolated hamlet for many years after this, and it remained a community outside the rule of law. The gangs owned or leased houses there and maintained warehousing facilities. Teams of horses were kept and carriers worked on a commission basis. Law-abiding citizens were coerced into accepting this situation, and might find contraband concealed on their own premises.

The London merchants came out to Stockwell, and sometimes to meeting places further afield, to strike the final bargain. A similar depot on Hounslow Heath served traffic coming from further west, and goods run on the Essex and Suffolk shores went to Epping Forest. Discretion dictated that the delivery to city storehouses was normally made by night, so that the convoys could be out again before daybreak, to return some ten days later with the next consignment. To cross the Thames at London Bridge was asking for trouble, and the smugglers evidently used the ferries at Lambeth and Battersea, or even bridges much further upstream at Putney or beside Hampton Court. Goods were stored in central London in some surprising places; there are records of tea being concealed in Berkley Mews and even within Fleet Prison. Uncustomed tobacco, which more often entered London by means of documentation fraud in the port, went for processing to the East End. One cigar manufacturer is reported to have entertained Customs officials while men in his warehouse were hastily removing the incriminating seals on 800lbs of tobacco and 350lbs of snuff. There is also the story of a youth who traced a waggon-load of 3000lbs of tobacco by its smell, and then blackmailed the driver!

In most business transactions, the biggest profits tend to be made in retailing and distribution, so it is not so surprising that the most powerful smuggling gangs grew up at key points on the network of routes into London. Hawkhurst is more than 13 miles from the nearest point on the coast, and the other gang headquarters were even further inland. (Mayfield is about 15 miles from the sea, Horsham 17, and Groombridge 21.) We can follow what must have been the typical operation organised from Hawkhurst around 1740. A large consignment of tea would be brought ashore at Bulverhythe near Hastings, loaded onto waiting packhorses and carried up through the woods of Hollington, to continue either through Battle or Sedlescombe. Turner, the landlord of an inn at Whatlington, was part of the organisation, and 'Turner's Hole' was a regular depot. We know from evidence given by a leading smuggler that such a load of tea could reach 'safe houses' on the southern fringe of London on the day after it had been brought ashore. However, if there were any delay, the Hawkhurst gang had a variety of other storage points: a barn at Hurst Green, a specially-built bonded store at Seacox Heath, Hawkhurst, or depots at Hartley, Angley, Sissinghurst, Cranbrook or Goudhurst, for example, and probably also at Pembury near Tonbridge.

We know the favourite route the Groombridge smugglers used from this point onwards through the disclosures made by an informer calling himself Goring. Anyone familiar with the countryside and place names along the North Downs near Sevenoaks may like to try a little detective work on the following extract which concerned a landing of tea at Bulverhythe in 1737. He writes: '... the Groombridge Smugglers were forced to carry their goods allmost all up to Rushmore Hill and Cester Mark [Keston Mark], which some they do now, and Chaps from London come down to Groombridge almost every day, as they used to do last winter...' That this was part of one of the main routes into London becomes clear from other references; about the same time 2855 pounds of tea were found hidden in a field beside Rushmore Hill.

Again in 1740 there is a story of a captured Exciseman taken by smugglers and held overnight at 'Sprats Bottom near Farnborow' (Pratts Bottom near Farnborough). These smugglers were unmistakably using part of the Rye Road, the first in Kent to be turnpiked, which led from London out through Sevenoaks. Anyone driving north down the long descent of the Sevenoaks Bypass, who has time to raise his eyes from the complexities of the M 25 interchange, will see where they went. A minor road still runs diagonally up the North Downs from Dunton Green to Knockholt and continues down Rushmore Hill, to join the A21 at Pratts Bottom. (The present line of the A21 over Polhill was built later to ease the gradient for coaches.) Other references concerning this route include the finding of goods worth £5000 at Woodsgate on this turnpike, and there are accounts of goods going through Sundridge and Plaxtead (evidently Plaxtol) nearby.

Jacob Pring, or Prim was the Hawkhurst man detailed to manage the London end of the business. He was living at Beckenham (then a small village about nine miles from the City). So the typical consignment of tea was carried towards London down Rushmore Hill, through Bromley and Beckenham to the depot at Stockwell, where the bargain was struck with City merchants. Incidentally on one occasion Jacob Pring was involved in an attack on a Custom House officer who was watching a cricket match on Bromley Common, and his victim had to take refuge in the almshouses at Bromley College!

We know the story of two actual smuggling convoys around 1740; neither is typical, if only because these were occasions which the authorities discovered. In June 1743 a load of tea and brandy was brought ashore between Bexhill and Pevensey. James Blackman, innkeeper at the village of Hooe, a short distance inland, escorted the armed and mounted convoy on its next stage to a hiding place in Ashdown Forest. At Wych Cross, the highest point on the road near Forest Row, the party stopped and unloaded. After resting there undisturbed, they moved off along what is now the A22, the newly turnpiked road through East Grinstead and Felbridge. At this point

the usual route continued into London via Ocalstrom, but this particular consignment was destined for other customers, and the convoy headed for the river crossing at Thames Ditton, to disappear in the direction of Watford.

The second story concerns tea brought ashore on the West Sussex coast at South Lancing. That landing had been organised by local men from the Steyning area under a farmer called Edward Sowton. The tea was taken for storage to Handcross in St Leonard's Forest, south of Crawley. It had been bought by Nicholas Hixon (who was either the buyer for a large concern or one of the smaller independent dealers). Hixon took his tea towards London, probably along what is now the A23, but was caught taking it in a cart across Putney Bridge.

Following his capture Nicholas Hixon was forced to disclose at least part of his activities. He came from Wickham, near Fareham in Hampshire (another regular smuggling centre). He had trading contacts with various smuggling concerns in West Sussex, and bought goods landed at Lancing and Littlehampton. He admitted buying brandy and tea from the innkeeper at Storrington; this was delivered to him 'at night under Boxhill between Dorking and Mickleham'. He named several other men who had been with him buying contraband near Steyning on one occasion in 1746. These included two local shopkeepers (a butcher from East Grinstead and victualler from Bramber), but also a man from Warminster in Wiltshire and Trip Stanford, who was a Hawkhurst gang member. He also admitted buying nearly 400 gallons of brandy at Shanklin Chine on the Isle of Wight, and paid the owner of a Cowes smuggling cutter for this, a considerable capital outlay!

The activities of men like Hixon and Jacob Pring show just how freely the smugglers and their associates moved around the countryside. When Jacob Pring later decided to save his own skin by betraying two other Hawkhurst men, he rode from Beckenham to Bristol to find them, brought them back to his home, and then rode to Horsham and back to ensure their capture! Those journeys would tax a modern driver's ability to read the road signs, but Jacob Pring was using shocking roads with very little to guide him. Moreover, at this time the Law of Settlement tied a labouring man to his parish for life! One might suspect that the Hawkhurst gang were subscribers to the excellent maps of Sussex produced by Richard Budgen in 1724!

The 'five and twenty ponies trotting through the dark', which provide the telling refrain in Rudyard Kipling's poem, call up an

A cartoon of 1813, showing Riding Officers searching a coach on the Dover Road. Reproduced by kind permission of HM Commissioners of Customs and Excise.

image which could well have been true in the late stages of the smuggling story, when discretion meant the need to switch from one route to another, but was certainly not so during the heyday of the trade. Especially around 1780, armed convoys of a hundred men or more left the Kent and Sussex coasts more regularly and frequently than the stage coaches, secure in their strength of numbers. The routes funnelled into London from East Kent via Canterbury or Faversham and Rochester. From Folkestone or Hythe one way was along the old Pilgrim road, to cross the Medway by the bridge at Aylesford (where the George Inn was a safe house); the alternative was the main road through Maidstone, and there were major storage facilities at Boxley and Wrotham. From Rye or Hastings most goods went via the Hawkhurst area and the Sevenoaks turnpike, as we have seen. Ashdown Forest provided excellent temporary storage for goods landed elsewhere in East Sussex. There are known to have been hiding places near the lakes in Sheffield Park, among well recognised clumps of trees and near the villages of Buxted, Fairwarp, Duddeswell and Nutley. Contraband landed in the Brighton and Worthing area often went north through Lindfield (where 300 laden horses were seen passing on one occasion in 1782), and the house and grounds of Gravetye Manor near East Grinstead were also used for concealment at times. Godstone, Tandridge and Oxted all figure in smuggling stories. Much of the contraband landed further west went first to the markets at Horsham, and was stored in St Leonard's Forest if necessary. Hawkin's Pond here was a meeting place, and a drunken smuggler was drowned when he blundered into it. One of the smaller convoys from Horsham was intercepted on Wimbledon Common in 1772, and the smugglers lost their goods and horses. Crawley and Copthorne were for a time local gang headquarters for goods heading for Reigate, and convoys from Chichester Harbour were often carried through Petersfield and Hindhead.

There was another quite different way to get contraband into London. For those with the right contacts the easiest method was by ship together with the legal cargo. Much could be achieved by false documents and mythical transfers of goods. An alternative strategy was to offload the goods within the Thames estuary or in the congested port itself. Every type of vessel took part; fishing boats, colliers and Thames barges brought in their quota beneath their legitimate cargo, but the biggest profits were to be made from large vessels trading with the East and West Indies. The fun usually began at Gravesend, and even naval ships were implicated. When HMS *Lyme* returned from Virginia in 1719, no Customs search was allowed below decks. It became customary for officials boarding a merchantman to chalk up what they looked for by way of a bribe, and the silent bargaining continued until agreement was reached. Henry Shore was able to quote from a private letter of 1833 to the effect that Gravesend Watermen were already on board ship to negotiate the distribution to small trading craft, and that the chartered merchantmen involved had disposed of goods worth £20,000 on the previous voyage. The East India Company's vessels berthed at Blackwall and escaped the worst pillage, for congestion within the Pool of London was notorious. In 1700 dutiable goods had to be landed on the Legal Quays, a mere 500 yards of river frontage between London Bridge and the Tower. The so-called Sufferance Wharfs on the opposite bank were then added, but the first docks were not built until after 1800. Vessels in the Pool or alongside the quays were jostled day and night by a motley collection of hopeful enthusiasts in small boats 'as people resorting to a fair. ... watching the opportunity to convey goods out of every porthole of the ship'.

If much of the contraband was taken to London, a lot went to supply more local needs. The most expensive items – fine wines, silk and other delicate fabrics – were probably brought in to order, for a discriminating clientele which may have included royalty. The clergy and substantial householders got their supplies through local dealers. Prudent housewives bought their tea from 'duffers' who carried it quilted into their caps and great coats, and had to keep a sharp eye on its quality and freedom from adulteration with hedgerow leaves. Parson Woodforde at his Norfolk rectory reveals in his diary that he bought his contraband from known agents, and was on one occasion allowed to sample the gin before placing an order. He felt justifiably distressed when a tub supplied in 1783 yielded a mere 18 bottles of spirit instead of the customary 20.

By 1820 the smuggling trade was fighting a losing battle against the preventive services, but there was still a ready market for its goods. Transport and travel might be easier, but it was now very much more dangerous for the smugglers. A Kent man, known to his associates as Old Sobers, remembered what it was like, and later told his reminiscences to City businessman John Terry. His story was first published (appropriately) in the City Press. Old Sobers must have been born around 1800. His family lived at Wrotham in Kent and were obviously prosperous; as he said 'we could muster 50 horses' and his father would change out of his working farmer's clothes and go in style by coach to meet his business contacts in the City. The family fortune was built round the transport of goods normally landed in Sandwich Bay, and sold to reputable City merchants in Wood Street. For successful operation this required good communications and Wrotham was well placed for this. Today it is at the junction of the M20 and M26, and immediately below a radio mast on the North

41

The Revenue cutter *Vigilant* towing a barge seized for carrying contraband tobacco, at Greenwich in 1749. Reproduced by kind permission of Alan Hay.

Downs crest. The Sobers family operated their own effective system. Coaches from Dover came by along the turnpike at least eight times a day, and, for a consideration, the guard would relay the news in terms of a tune on his trumpet. *The girl I left behind me* meant the Preventives are out by the sea! Cows in the fields above the village were then tethered in groups of three, or if it were dark, a light appeared in a particular window. When the 'all clear' came, the men of Platt, Wrotham and Ightham collected their two hundred horses and set off. They were a strong enough force to resist trouble but, as Sobers said, it was the smaller landing parties who got caught by the press gang. Apparently even in 1820 the Mayor of Deal could be relied on to take the smugglers' side, and the Excisemen of Sandwich would sit catching eels with absorbed concentration.

The family dealt in silks, lace, tobacco and spirits, and had a City agent for each commodity. There were numerous depots and hiding places locally, in Mereworth Woods, among the sandpits and quarries near Borough Green, and at Oldbury Camp (the Iron Age entrenchment at Ightham). Huge stacks of wood were particularly useful, and at the age of 17, Old Sobers would take a load of brooms to London by cart, stay at the Cross Keys near Mitre Court, and return with £1000! Like his brothers he had been trained for the business from an early age (they had a shooting range for practice). When only 13 he would be sent alone at midnight, and by dog cart, with a message for someone in 'the marsh'. As a young man he went to Flushing to be the family agent and buyer there.

After 1826 everything went wrong; one brother ended in Australia, another did penal service in the navy, and there were heavy fines all round. The family fortune collapsed (though partly for reasons unconnected with their change in business affairs). To add insult to injury, a government semaphore station now operated from the summit of Wrotham Hill. Like many other men who had tasted wealth and adventure, Old Sobers was left with his reminiscences!

4
The North Kent Coast from Gravesend to Pegwell Bay

The north Kent coast illustrates a great variety of smuggling methods and personalities. For two short periods it became a battleground for major gangs, but for much of the time smaller organisations carried on the trade, with a fair degree of connivance from those employed to prevent it. Among the leading personalities are the flamboyant Joss Snelling of Broadstairs, the discreet Dr Rutton of Seasalter and the hypocritical Rev Thomas Patten of Whitstable. Moreover, there are two quite different types of coastline in north Kent, and accordingly the story of what happened here divides naturally into two sections. The more typical episodes, involving gangs running goods ashore on open beaches, took place along the coast eastwards from Seasalter and Whitstable round Thanet and into Sandwich Bay. The opportunities within the muddy waters of the Thames estuary were distinctly different; characteristically too we know very much less about what took place here.

The best prospects in the Thames Estuary lay either in offloading part of a cargo from vessels engaged in legitimate trade, or else in small scale ventures which could be carried out unobserved within the narrow channels and creeks. The shores of the Hoo Peninsula and Isle of Grain to the west of the Medway, Stangate Creek, the Isle of Sheppey and the creeks at Sittingbourne, Conyer and Faversham to the east, were the regular landing sites. Charles Dickens was to describe this landscape, when prison hulks and plague ships were anchored offshore, in the opening chapters of *Great Expectations*. (A pathetic row of small tombstones in the churchyard at Cooling on the Hoo Peninsula is believed to have inspired part of the story.) During the smuggling years these marshes were still malarial; even today it is easy to visualise the landscape the smugglers knew. This is particularly true at the extremely isolated Shades House in Halstow Marshes

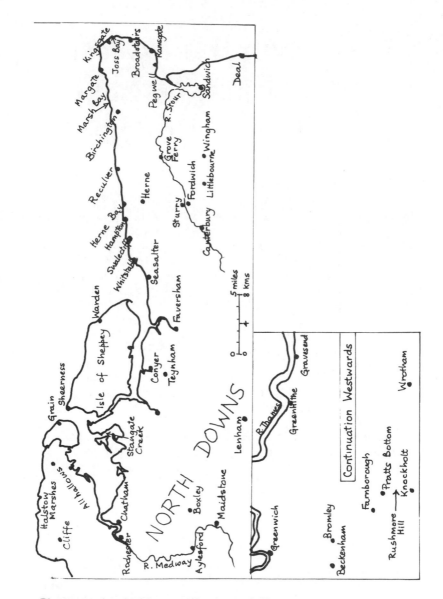

Places associated with smuggling in north Kent.

north of Cooling, among old farm buildings near Allhallows or at the Hogarth Inn on the Isle of Grain, and all have known associations with the trade. Equally evocative is the small wharf at Conyer, west of Faversham. This was regularly used by the smuggling community at nearby Teynham, and the boatyard and Ship Inn at Conyer are strong reminders of this lawless past.

The story of one small scale enterprise, which must have been typical of many more, concerns the Roots family of Chatham. Edward Roots, his brother Richard and several other local men formed a consortium to bring goods from Flushing and Ostend during the 1720s. Londoner Thomas Pigmore put up the capital, and Edward Roots owned a vessel called the *Mermaid* which could carry about 500 lbs of tea on each trip. Between September 1727 and June 1728 they managed ten voyages, landing cargoes on the Hoo peninsula, which then had a preventive force of a mere two Riding Officers. On five occasions they used Chalk Marshes (close to Gravesend) and a hide near Chalk church. They also used Cliffe Marshes, and hid goods near Higham, and twice risked using quays in the Medway. The goods were then taken on horseback to 'Yorkshire Tom' (the Duke of Montague's gardener at Blackheath) who met them on Blackheath or Shooters Hill, and the tea was finally sold in the alehouses of Deptford at 10/- a pound. This profitable business survived the seizure of the *Mermaid*; Edward Roots bought another vessel and continued trading.

Sheppey (which means the island of sheep) was notorious as a centre of the owling trade, although few details of what took place here appear to have survived. Henry Baker, who had overall responsibility for the preventive forces, reported in 1698 that a beach on the north east of the island could be used at almost all stages of the tide, and the men working the three ferries which linked Sheppey to the mainland acted as lookouts to warn of any opposition. In 1745 a gang stole wool worth the huge sum of £1500 from a farm near Sheerness. A week later eight men were arrested as they tried to ship out part of their prize. There was still no Excise Officer on Sheppey during the lawless 1780s, and it was then believed that the Revenue was losing £60,000 a year from contraband traffic here and in the Medway estuary.

The Thames marshes lay within the customs control of the port of Rochester, and a desperate official was to describe the situation around 1740 as an infestation of smugglers. Officers were assaulted and fines for minor offences went unpaid. Part of the trouble came from goods shipped directly into the Medway, and one informer spoke of five cutters, able to bring in between them six tons of tea and 2000 tubs of spirit in a week. There was also smuggling out of vessels

Part of the smugglers' beach at Whitstable, with the Isle of Sheppey in the distance.

held in quarantine at Stangate Creek, near the Medway mouth. But a great deal of contraband passing through Rochester along the Roman road had been landed on beaches much further to the east. This was a continuing problem throughout the smuggling years; at its worst around 1780 when armed convoys rode through every few days.

The ancient port and market town of Faversham was equally notorious. Dutch oyster boats and local vessels brought goods up Faversham Creek (some had sailed right round Sheppey to avoid detection). Supplies also came from the beaches between Seasalter and Reculver, and were regularly and openly sold in the market below the fine timber-framed Guildhall. When Daniel Defoe came here in 1724, the main feature was still the owling trade, and he commented on the fortunes to be made by this. The many fine houses (often with Georgian facades masking an earlier structure) are an indication of the prosperity brought by trade, both legitimate and otherwise. The local community invariably sided with the smugglers. At a time when known free traders were outlawed during the 1740s, a Faversham smuggler called Millaway confessed to a local Justice of the Peace that some years previously he had shot an Exciseman; nevertheless he went free!

Faversham stood at the western extremity of the major smuggling beaches. From Seasalter round to Sandwich Day there were immeasurable opportunities for illicit trading on a coast relatively sheltered from prevailing winds and tantalisingly close to continental suppliers. The oyster fishermen of Seasalter and Whitstable, and the seamen of the Thanet ports had an intimate knowledge of the whole coastline, and sometimes had family links with the Low Countries. Around 1700 a gang of a dozen Frenchmen were living in Canterbury alongside Walloon wool combers, and were well placed to ship out wool from flocks on the rich coastal pastures nearby. Continental clothiers came to rely on the fine quality product they knew as 'Canterbury Wool'. Apart from the small ports of Whitstable, Margate, Broadstairs and Ramsgate, the farms and hamlets then lay inland, leaving an empty shoreline and sandy beaches accessible but happily unobserved, at least until the late eighteenth century. Where the coast was backed by cliffs (of unstable clay near Herne but chalk on Thanet) it was easy to construct trackways leading inland. The Blean woodlands behind what later became Herne Bay were particularly useful hiding places on routes to the markets at Canterbury and Faversham. The recognised alternative route ran through Grove Ferry and Fordwich inland.

The coastal cliffs provided caves for storage and divided up the shoreline into separate bays, a particularly striking feature along the coasts of Thanet. Here generations of local people improved access to the beaches below the soft chalk cliffs by excavating stairways and steep canyon-like cartways. The older villages stood back from the coast – St Lawrence behind Ramsgate, St Peter's and Reading Street behind Broadstairs – and it was from these villages that farm tracks radiated out towards the various gaps and gates where the shore could be reached. Much later these were to become the roads round which the modern housing estates have developed, but in the eighteenth century each provided an enterprising landowner with discreet access to his own beach, and caves for storage. Today's holiday makers know them well: Sackett's Gap down to Palm Bay, Foreness Stairs and Kemp's Stairs to Botany Bay, Kingsgate itself, and at Broadstairs, Stone Gap, Waterloo Stairs and Dumpton Gap. In their day each must have proved a veritable goldmine, and some of the older farmhouses, resplendent with Flemish gables, bear witness to this prosperity. Margate, Broadstairs and Ramsgate were small fishing ports at this time, but had once held the privilege of exemption from customs dues as minor members of the Cinque Ports Confederation. When Daniel Defoe came to Broadstairs in 1723 (then known as Bradstowe), he noted that only a small fraction of the inhabitants appeared to be supported by legitimate activities, and he found it unwise to inquire too closely how most people lived!

49

It was probably because the landing beaches were often relatively restricted, even near Herne and Whitstable, that smuggling tended to be carried on by a number of small local gangs. And since smuggler and preventiveman had to live side by side, there are clear signs that a degree of quiet accommodation was worked out which left both sides better off. We may suspect that this was the case at the ancient village of Herne, clustered round the fine medieval church of St Martin on a hillside a short distance above what is now Herne Bay. Around 1700 Herne was home to both a smuggling community and the local Riding Officer; it lay on one of the main routes from the coast into Canterbury, and storage facilities were presently developed both in the village and at nearby farms. The Herne smugglers had direct access to beaches at Hampton, Herne Bay, Bishopstone and Reculver. The first Riding Officer based at Herne was Francis Pilcher, and in 1698 he was awarded £40 for seizing a parcel of wool as it was being shipped out. Two officers who succeeded him reported that they were being threatened by local smugglers. Despite this intimidation William Eads, who was Riding Officer at Herne in the 1730s, became sufficiently wealthy to have a vote in Parliament (an achievement which could hardly have come from his official salary of £25 a year!) On the other side, William Chamberlain of Herne was leader of the local wool smugglers. In ten years he too rose from poverty to become a substantial freeholder who could also claim a parliamentary vote.

By 1730 the main activity had become the landing of tea and spirits, but this had not yet developed into a major industry or been backed up by armed force. The local Petty Sessions record numerous minor cases. The fine for selling contraband tea was apparently three times its legal value, and one of the largest fines recorded was for £200 on Edward Goatham, a victualler at Ramsgate, for selling uncustomed spirits. This situation changed rapidly once the large gangs moved in around 1740. A gang based at Wingham and their notorious associates from Hawkhurst now began to use some of the larger beaches near Margate and Reculver. Much later the Rev Richard Barham (who had personal experience of what went on) was to set his poem *The Smuggler's Leap* at Reculver, with a graphic account of a typical run.

In March 1744 Mr Ketcherell, Supervisor at Canterbury, wrote to his superior John Collier to alert him to the increasingly serious situation. He explained that gangs taking goods to London stopped in Canterbury almost daily, and that they regularly spent one or two days in Thanet. He instanced a gang who had spent a whole day in Birchington, each man armed with a pair of pistols and a blunderbuss. Local officials everywhere faced threats and intimidation, and farmers were browbeaten into supplying horses and feed. This viol-

The smuggling beach beside the Blue Anchor Inn at Seasalter.

ence increased partly because, as one bitter official pointed out, there had been no Revenue vessel on patrol offshore for months. In April 1746, following the landing of 11½ tons of tea in Sandwich Bay, the Hawkhurst men turned on their associates from Wingham and took away their horses. It was believed the same Hawkhurst men then went on to rescue some nine tons of tea which had been seized at Margate. In the months which followed there were reports of two hundred men passing through St Peters, and of other major landings at Reculver and Kingsgate. In March 1747 a ton of tea and quantities of coffee, cambric, linen and firearms were captured and held in Margate, and it took the combined forces of all the preventive services of Thanet and Sandwich, with naval help, to prevent recapture.

In 1714 Mr Ketcherell sent another telling account to John Collier. 130 men had landed a cargo between Reculver and Birchington; they then split into two parties, 63 men and 80 or 90 horses went via Herne Bay and Faversham (where they were seen by one official who recognised some of them but did not know their names), and the rest followed the alternative route via Grove Ferry and Canterbury. Part of this information had been passed on to Mr Ketcherell by the Rev Thomas Patten of Whitstable. His parsonage stood beside the shore at Seasalter, and apparently he dabbled in smuggling himself. Moreover, he was accustomed to levying a tithe on local contraband, 51 as on all other production! But this group, whom he described as 'such rugged colts' refused to comply, and the Rev Patten felt justified in reporting their conduct. Later accounts confirmed that members of the Hawkhurst gang were responsible for these violent episodes. Jeremiah Curtis was named in connection with an armed struggle at Epple Bay, Birchington, and John Munton of Sittingbourne and other known gang members assembled at Chislet for a landing at Reculver, just to the north. Fortunately for the people of north Kent, the Hawkhurst gang was broken shortly after this, and the local communities reverted to quieter tactics.

Seasalter was the heart of another smuggling organisation whose very existence has only recently been revealed through detailed work by Wallace Harvey. Seasalter takes its name from the old-established salt works there. In the early eighteenth century it was a small fishing community on the edge of marshes, yet for more than a century the lease of Seasalter Parsonage Farm (immediately above the shore) was held by a succession of well-established gentlemen who came from outside the area. The farm was occupied by their nominees, men who took on relatively arduous and ill-paid employment in the customs service as Riding Officers, Coastwaiters and Tide Surveyors, but who then retired to settle down as bankers, builders and lawyers. In all Mr Harvey has traced some sixteen men, all of whom made a very

Seasalter Parsonage Farm in Genesta Avenue, which became the operational headquarters of a smuggling company in 1740.

handsome living in no very obvious fashion. The details of their web of relationships within an organisation which was perhaps controlled from Dover, are too complicated to be readily summarised, but it is worth looking at the known facts about two key members. Incidentally not one of them was caught doing wrong, though one was certainly suspected, and was for a time removed from his post as local Riding Officer and Coastwaiter.

The founder member of what Mr Harvey calls the Seasalter Company was Dr Isaac Rutton of Ashford, who leased Seasalter Parsonage Farm in 1740. At this stage the contraband was brought ashore beside the Blue Anchor Inn and stored at local farms if necessary. Pink Farm in Seasalter Lane was one of these, and when it was demolished in 1953, a secret room was discovered behind a door disguised as a cupboard, also accessible by a shaft from a windowless room above. There were later stories of ditches temporarily filled with tubs, and haystacks which suddenly doubled in size and reeked of tobacco! The pack horse convoys headed for Blue House Farm on the North Downs above Lenham, and the road to London. They used the old byways south of the present main road (A299), and continued up Brogdale Road and through White Hill. To ensure a safe passage, Dr Rutton installed his eldest son first at White Hill and then at Chapel House, Ospringe (which stood above a spacious crypt!). His other son was vicar of a local parish. The need to bring horses to fresh marsh pastures masked the necessary movement of pack animals, and it would have been an easy matter for contraband to be picked up at Lenham and taken on towards London.

Dr Rutton, his sons and associates all benefited handsomely from their unspecified activities at Seasalter, as the company continued trading through the eighteenth century, but it was Mr William Baldock who reaped the richest rewards. He began life in extremely modest circumstances, looking after cows. From builder's labourer he graduated to managing a Whitstable inn, and then to owning a sailing vessel. By 1776 he was advertising the services of two ships which regularly sailed from Whitstable to London and back, and he soon began buying and renting out land. By 1792 he was living in Canterbury in some style, as a Justice of the Peace and owner of St Dunstan's Brewery. At this point Dr Rutton died, and his sons assigned the unexpired lease of Seasalter Parsonage Farm to William Baldock. The changes he brought to the organisation deserve further consideration later; at this stage it is appropriate to report that when he died in 1812, this erstwhile cowherd had amassed £1,100,000!

Along the cliffed coast of East Thanet another individualist was building up his smuggling empire. The seamen of Broadstairs and the villagers of St Peters and Reading Street continued to depend on the trade as they had done when Defoe made his enquiries in 1723. A favourite landing place was Stone Gap, just north of Broadstairs. Stone House, which still stands on the corner of Lanthorne Road, dates from the late seventeenth century, when it was a farmhouse surrounded by outbuildings. A large tunnel leading down to the sea was accidentally rediscovered when a bulldozer clearing a building site fell into it in 1954. There were recognised storage sites nearby in Elmwood Road (where one at least of the caves beside the road was used in this way), and also in Reading Street and St Peters. This was the territory in which Joss Snelling became leader of a local gang. He was born at St Peters in 1741, and survived the hazards of his profession to die peacefully in 1837. Indeed he was still smuggling on Thanet in his ninetieth year! Presumably he took his name from a favourite landing site in Joss Bay; he lived in Lanthorne Road at Callis Court Cottage (now Farm Cottage), and recruited extra help, when required, at the Fig Tree Inn in Callis Court Road.

Many of his activities went unrecorded, but in 1769 his gang became involved in what became known as the Battle of Botany Bay. This began in the early hours of a spring morning on the shore between Kingsgate and Foreness Point further north. Joss Snelling and his men had almost completed the unloading of a vessel when they were challenged by a patrol led by an Excise officer. In the fight which followed ten smugglers were fatally injured and eight were captured. Joss Snelling and four other men escaped up Kemp's Stairs onto the clifftop, only to be challenged by the local Riding Officer. They promptly shot him and fled inland to Reading Street, while he was carried into the parlour of the Captain Digby Inn at Kingsgate, where he died. The house-to-house search of Reading Street which followed revealed one dead smuggler and another seriously injured, but Joss himself got away. For a time his gang was severely depleted, but he went on to a lifetime in the trade, eventually recruiting his son and grandson into the business. He was even presented to the future Queen Victoria as the famous Broadstairs smuggler! His activities have been chronicled by Mr W H Lapthorne, and are now commemorated in the smuggling museum at Bleak House in Broadstairs.

Meanwhile other developments in north Kent had an influence on the pattern of smuggling. Margate was becoming one of the first coastal resorts. Sea bathing had begun here in the 1720s but the bathing machine was not perfected until thirty years later. Thereafter visitors could at times watch signals being exchanged between a clifftop lookout and a vessel offshore. A gardener working behind a house off Trinity Square in central Margate fell to his death through the roof of a series of caverns whose presence had long been forgotten. The householder found an immediate use for storage facilities close to

The beach once used by the Hawkhurst gang at Reculver in Kent. Coastal erosion destroyed the ancient church, which stands within the Roman fort and beside Coastguard cottages.

the seafront, as visitors to the Smugglers' Caves of Margate can see today!

Higher customs dues and fewer preventivemen led everywhere to an expansion of smuggling during the 1780s. The best known episode from this time took place in February 1780, when the local Excise Supervisor was taking a load of captured gin from Whitstable to Canterbury with an escort of nine soldiers. Where the road climbs steeply out of Whitstable (towards the roundabout at the crossing with the A299) fifty-three smugglers caught and attacked the convoy. They killed two soldiers and wounded others, before escaping with the gin. Retribution followed, and 18-year-old John Knight was tried and executed at Maidstone. His body was hung in chains on Bostall Hill as a warning to others.

During the long years of the war with France between 1793 and 1815 barracks were built, defences strengthened and signal stations set up along the Kent coast. The older houses along the seafront in Herne Bay were built mainly for officers and their families, when the West Kent Regiment was stationed here. The Swalecliffe and Whitstable smugglers now found a new and highly profitable line of business in shipping out French prisoners-of-war. Their oyster boats made regular and frequent trips to the London markets, and also main-

55

Joss Snelling, the Broadstairs smuggler, outside Callis Court Cottage, where he lived. Reproduced by kind permission of W H Lapthorne.

tained invaluable contacts with Flushing, Dunkirk and Ostend. For large numbers of desperate French prisoners, kept manacled and in hideous conditions on hulks moored along the Thames estuary, this represented the best hope of escape. Men jumped into the river, feigning suicide, and held on to the anchor chains while almost totally submerged. If relatives had sent the necessary ransom money, a waggon might be there to meet a prisoner and take him on to a Kent port. Other men found their way as best they could. Pye Alley Farm (on the A290 at the foot of Clapham Hill two miles from Seasalter) was a key point on the escape route. From here the Frenchmen struggled along the valley of the Bogshole Brook to reach the sea and embark on a vessel partly hidden by a shingle bank at Swalecliffe. When an old house in Castle Road, Whitstable was demolished forty years ago, a huge quantity of rusty iron manacles was found beneath the floor, probably left after a gang of men chained together had been landed on the offshore shingle bank known as The Street.

The Seasalter Company continued its discreet and profitable activities. By the time William Baldock took over the lease of Seasalter Parsonage Farm in 1792, he could make use of the new Canterbury turnpike, and divert the contraband traffic to his brewery at St Dunstan's, using horses and carts hired from local farmers. The route up to the turnpike on Pean Hill was along well screened byways via Fox's Cross, and there were hides in Ellenden Woods, but the summit of Pean Hill was dangerously exposed. Accordingly two houses with stabling were built, and 'signal stations' were established to link Canterbury with Whistable. These centred on Honey Hill Farm and messages were passed by raising or lowering a besom, and it was claimed that a warning could reach Whitstable before the oncoming preventive party had left the outskirts of Canterbury! William Baldock had little to fear on the coast; his nominee lived in Seasalter Parsonage Farm and his nephew was the local Riding Officer! Contraband for local customers travelled under loads of timber and bark from Ellenden Woods. The company's legal affairs were being managed by Edward Knocker, who had already done his stint at the Parsonage Farm, and presently became Town Clerk of Dover!

There were other family businesses operating in the Herne area. At Hampton, just west of Herne Bay, a headland projected seawards and sheltered a small pier used by local oyster boats. This was the preferred landing site of the Mount family of Hampton. The mouth of Bishopstone Glen, just east of Herne Bay, was another useful beach then favoured by Thomas Hancock's gang. He made and lost a fortune during his lifetime between 1774 and 1840. He was a shrewd investor and put his money into property, owning houses in Hunters Forstal Road and Reculver Road at Herne. He then rashly sold off contraband without telling the rest of his gang. They retaliated and burned his barn; later they blackmailed him and he was forced to sell off most of his land in order to placate them.

The crucial development which coincided with the return of the soldiers and sailors after Waterloo was the establishment of the Coast Blockade. By 1718 this had been extended to cover all the north Kent coasts east of Sheerness. The small companies of seamen, based in Watch Houses little more than a mile apart along key beaches, posed real problems for the smugglers. The Blockade sentinels were obvious targets for attack. In 1818 two men from the Broadstairs Watch House fell over the cliff and one was killed. This could have been an accident, or something more deliberate. There is no record that the Seasalter Company suffered from interference by the Blockade, though it happens that one surviving Watch House still stands beside the shore a mile west of Seasalter.

For a short period around 1820 there was a resurgence of violence, as the local smugglers and a more determined group from the Wingham and Canterbury areas attempted to maintain their trade. Using the old tactics of a large landing party flanked by armed men, this north Kent gang ran goods ashore at Reculver, Herne Bay and Stangate Creek (in the Medway estuary) during 1820, and another violent landing took place at Hampton in March 1821. The smugglers tied up the sentinel of the Watch House, which stood where Albany Road reaches the Herne Bay seafront. A few weeks later men from the same Watch House were involved in a more serious battle. Some sixty men, led by James West, a thatcher from Littlebourne near Canterbury, had assembled at Grove Ferry and collected arms there. The plan was to converge on the coast by two separate routes and hide in a meadow behind the shore at Herne Bay (near what is now the Queen's Hotel). The two groups would then get into position on either side of the landing. When the boat came ashore at 2.45 a.m., a patrol under midshipman Snow surprised the party. Snow challenged the smugglers and drew his pistol, but it misfired and he fell, fatally wounded. He was carried into the Ship Inn, and a surgeon was summoned, but his life could not be saved; he was later buried at Herne with full military honours. Meanwhile five smugglers had been captured, and three were to turn king's evidence. Nevertheless at the Old Bailey trial which followed, the accused were judged not guilty. However, when the same gang were caught at St Mildred's Bay in Thanet six months later, justice prevailed. Of the eighteen on trial, three were hanged and the rest faced transportation.

From this point on concealment and deception were essential. In 1822 when officers were searching a Margate house, they found a tunnel leading out from the cellar and running some 300 yards to a

Smugglers surprised at Kingsgate, Thanet in 1814, a drawing by Riding Officer Alan Harper, who is thought to have been an eye witness. Reproduced by kind permission of W H Lapthorne.

camouflaged opening on the beach. What is more, they found a man on his knees inside! Their estimate was that it must have taken 18 months to excavate, and cost £200. As late as 1850 Coastguards reported their suspicions that repeated runs were using an undiscovered tunnel from the beach to clifftop limekilns at what is now Cliftonville. Most episodes concerned tubs skilfully sunk offshore or concealed under cargoes of coal delivered to Sheerness. Skeins of tubs were left bobbing offshore and some broke loose, to become entangled in the legs of the new Herne Bay Pier. Some were found concealed within Ramsgate Harbour, and others in a barge off Birchington, protected by layers of planking and sand, and a cargo of wood three feet deep. In April 1830 Joss Snelling of Broadstairs was caught at his old tricks in St Mildred's Bay, and later fined £100.

By the time the Coastguard service had taken over from the Blockade in 1831 most men had been deterred by the likelihood of capture. The Seasalter Company, now led by William Hyder, apparently managed to reach an accommodation with the local men, who allowed themselves to be decoyed away at the crucial moment. Finally in 1845 the Coastguards of Herne Bay area felt able to report that the free trade had been extinguished. There remained one more bizarre episode. In 1851 (more than forty years after Britain had abolished the slave trade) an armed vessel boarded off Whitstable was found to be equipped as a slaver, with strings of beads for barter. However, since the boat was American-owned it was not possible to detain her!

PLACES TO VISIT

The Coast
The specially signed long distance *Saxon Shore Way* runs from Gravesend to Rye in Sussex, and passes Cliffe Marshes, Conyer Creek and other smuggling sites. (Leaflets from Kent Rights of Way Council, 2 London Rd, Faversham.)

Joss Bay and Kingsgate Bay, Thanet
The most scenic area to explore. Only public carpark off the B2052 at Joss Bay. Kingsgate was named to commemorate the landing of Charles II and his brother James when rough seas drove them ashore in 1683. A stone gateway was later built over the narrow gap down to the beach (now re-erected in nearby convent grounds). Kingsgate Castle and other gothic structures were built by Lord Holland, who owned the estate in the 1860s. Caves used for storage can be seen, and the Coastguard cottages which replaced the Blockade Watch House here. The Riding Officer killed during the Battle of Botany Bay of 1769 died in the Captain Digby Inn. From here a footpath leads north to Foreness Point, passing Kemp's Stairs (where Joss Snelling made his escape). South of Joss Bay are other points of interest. The present North Foreland Lighthouse is the successor to one erected in 1634. Just beyond here is Lanthorne Road. Despite high walls you can still see Stone House on the corner, and Joss Snelling's former home (now Farm Cottage) halfway along the north side of Lanthorne Road. In central Broadstairs are several old houses off Harbour Street with cellars and hiding places. When Charles Dickens stayed at Bleak House, he could watch local smugglers at work below Stone Gap, and a smugglers' museum in the basement now tells something of the story.

Other Visits

Seasalter and Whitstable
The beach at the Blue Anchor Inn (with carpark) and Seasalter Parsonage Farm in Genesta Avenue, close to the Rose in Bloom Inn at Seasalter have the strongest associations with smuggling. Wallace Harvey's two books give details of other places intimately linked to the trade. A mile west of the Blue Anchor on the coast at TR 069649 is

the Coast Blockade Watch House (now called Old Coastguard Cottage). Before the sea defences were built, this looked out directly onto the shore. In Whitstable itself the narrow street called Island Wall, which runs from the Oyster Company offices to the Neptune Inn, is at the heart of the smugglers' territory.

Herne and Herne Bay
At Herne village the best starting point is the very fine medieval church. Midshipman Snow is buried just west of the tower. The Smugglers Inn and Smugglers Cottages opposite may well have been associated with the trade. A little higher up the hill and set back to the left is a building known as Box Iron, from its original shape. When water mains were laid here in 1907, workmen came on a honeycomb of arched cellars, approached by an interior staircase. A passage led out to the side of the road, where there was a trapdoor and chains for lowering barrels. There were also cellars under the road itself.

At Herne Bay the most immediate link with a violent past is the Ship Inn on the seafront, where Midshipman Snow was fatally injured. Further along the seafront towards the pier is the Diver's Arms, built in 1836 by William Hooper Wood, a smuggler who returned from five years penal service in the navy to become a successful salvage diver. On two occasions he was found to have dug a convenient passage linking the inn cellars with the culvert taking the town brook to the sea! Herne Bay Library has a grappling device used for creeping up tubs.

Reculver
Here the main points of interest are the surviving portion of the Roman fort, built to protect ships in the Wantsum Channel, and the ruin of the twelfth century church, which contains fragments from a Saxon foundation. The site has been menaced over the centuries by coastal erosion, and most recently by a sea of caravans. The smuggling beaches are still there!

Pegwell Village
The village was a notorious haunt of smugglers in the eighteenth century but later became an elegant small resort, famous for its shrimp paste. The sea has destroyed steps down to the beach and the pier where regattas were once held. A smugglers' tunnel leading from the Belle View Tavern has now been blocked up. Much contraband

61

was landed in Pegwell Bay and taken up through an arched tunnel to the clifftop. A brooding line of Coastguard cottages built to control the situation after 1831, stands directly over caves the smugglers used for storage.

5

The East Kent Coast from Sandwich Bay to Fairlight Head

The most notorious smuggling coasts of Britain during the eighteenth century were in east Kent, and in particular those bordering on Romney Marsh. Some reasons for this are obvious; the Kent shores lay nearest to continental suppliers and many of the beaches were ideal for undisturbed landings. Wool from huge flocks of sheep on the marshes could be shipped over to France within days of a shearing, whatever the law might say. But in addition the economy of Kent around 1700 was depressed. Iron smelting at Wealden centres such as Lamberhurst, and the cloth-making industry of Tenterden and Cranbrook were dying. The harbours of the ancient and once proud Cinque Ports Confederation had been closed by mud and shingle. Sandwich, New Romney and Winchelsea had already lost their seaborne trade, and the haven at Hythe was finally abandoned in 1674. At Rye the citizens were to spend £60,000 in an unsuccessful bid to develop a new harbour, begun by John Smeaton in 1769 but abandoned in 1788. Inevitably there was a desperate need for alternative employment; exporting wool to continental clothiers proved profitable and easy, despite the fact that after 1662 this was a felony, at times punishable by death. Large scale importing of contraband came later, and initially as a means of paying for the wool.

As the two-way trade developed, the seamen of Deal, Dover and Folkestone crewed the smuggling vessels, while labourers in the countryside around were readily recruited as landers and porters. Until the preventive services were fully organised, the best landing sites were the long stretches of sand and shingle which began in the north with the wide sweep of Sandwich Bay. Here waterside Deal had grown up in the seventeenth century specifically to serve ships waiting in The Downs. The great crescent of shoals known as the Goodwin Sands, though the graveyard of so many vessels, provided a sheltered 63

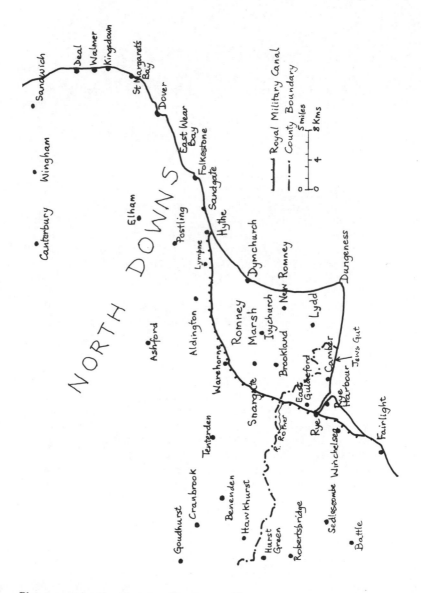

Places associated with smuggling in east Kent.

anchorage for sailing ships awaiting a favourable wind, and Deal seamen rowed out with messages and fresh supplies, using boats launched from their shingle beach. They also went to the help of ships in distress. In the great storm of 1703, when 16 naval vessels and 40 other ships foundered off the Goodwins with the loss of 2168 lives, the seamen of Deal saved 200 men. Unfortunately they also acquired a considerable reputation as hovellers (looters) and smugglers. In particular, they were adept at trading with vessels homeward bound from the East and West Indies. So much was being 'lost' in this way that it became normal practice for vessels belonging to the East India Company to be escorted through the Straits of Dover and up the Thames to London.

The open beaches of Sandwich Bay were ideal landing sites, and the smaller St Margaret's Bay and Langdon and Fan Bays further south were also used, although the surrounding chalk cliffs made these less accessible. At Dover itself the harbour mouth opened to the west of the town; it was patently rash to land a cargo on the beach east of this, under the eyes of the castle garrison and close to the gaol and Custom House. Nevertheless smuggling ships did come into the port, and at times goods were taken up the cliffs west of the harbour, and at Lydden Spout.

The most popular beaches began at East Wear Bay, beside what was then the small fishing village of Folkestone, and continued round past Sandgate and Hythe, and along the three-mile artificial embankment known as Dymchurch Wall. Here the core of the sea defences is thought to be Roman, but it has been strengthened and increased in height at various periods since (most recently after the sea surge of 1953). Strictly speaking, Romney Marsh is the northern section only of the triangular lowland running out to Dungeness. It had been reclaimed from the sea by Roman times. Rhee Wall, which forms its southern boundary and carries the road from New Romney to Appledore, was probably a natural feature which the Romans built up further. This provided the most direct route by which contraband could be carried inland towards Tenterden, High Halden, Biddenden and Cranbrook (all notorious smuggling centres). However, a particular advantage here was the way the smugglers could outwit pursuit by using local people as pilots through the maze of drainage ditches. Another advantage was the way the shores of the marsh faced two different directions, and so gave a choice of landing site, according to the prevailing wind.

South of Dymchurch the coastline in 1700 differed substantially from the present one. All that remained of the harbour which had once served the Cinque Port of New Romney was a shallow bay, opening to the sea between the markers of Littlestone and Greatstone.   65

SMUGGLING IN KENT AND SUSSEX

The Woolpack Inn at Warehorne above Romney Marsh. There is a tunnel to the church from the cellars, and this is one of several inns associated with the owling trade.

Lydd had grown along a shingle bank which was once virtually an island, and still retained its contact with the sea. As at Deal, the seamen of Lydd launched their small boats over greased timbers direct from the beach. The present Pilot Inn, on the road to Dungeness, is the successor to a much older inn of the same name, for it was common for vessels to take on a pilot here before entering the Straits of Dover. It was equally common for the boat taking the pilot out to return with useful items from its cargo! Walland Marsh, south of Rhee Wall, had mainly been reclaimed during the medieval period, and the parallel roads and tracks (particularly near Brookland) are the result of a succession of 'innings'. The extremely sharp bend on the A259 at the county boundary (Kent Ditch) is one of the points where carts waited for the men carrying goods across the most recently reclaimed marsh behind Camber. The favourite landing sites along the southern coast of the marsh were at Jew's Gut (now Jury's Gut) just east of Camber, and the sandy beach at Camber itself, where the dunes gave good cover for men awaiting a landing.

Rye and Winchelsea were separated from the marsh both by the county boundary and the wide tidal estuary of the river Rother, but shared much of its way of life. In 1700 Rye was still a seaport, with commercial quays on its west flank and the fishermen's quarter below the cliffs to the east. There was no bridge linking Rye to the marsh throughout the smuggling years. Instead a ferry ran across to East Guldeford (where every house was said to be an owler's). The ferry-man's house at Rye has survived, and can still be seen near the river bank among the boatyards, below Ypres Tower.

South of Rye the smuggling shores continued along Pett Level to the cliffs at Fairlight. Contemporary maps show that carts could be taken down to the beach at Fairlight Cove (immediately east of the village) and also at the foot of Fairlight Glen. Some accounts of smuggling here distinguish between episodes at 'Fairlight Steps', and those in Covehurst or Govers Bay. Both were certainly used, particularly by the owlers, but coastal erosion and large landslides have since substantially altered the coast here, making the former inaccessible and the other beach difficult to reach on foot.

This is the background against which the different phases of the smuggling story in east Kent were to unfold. From 1680 to 1720 the interest is focused on the owling trade in the marsh and the activities of the Mayfield gang. By 1730 the main development was the rise of other major gangs, particularly that based at Hawkhurst. Fifty years later it was the sea smugglers, and especially the men of Deal who most worried the government. The final phase is essentially the story of the Coast Blockade, and the activities of the last short-lived gang based at Aldington. So strongly were the preventive services organised here that smuggling was virtually extinguished by 1830.

The attempts to stop wool smuggling from east Kent began well before 1700. William Carter, who was a clothier, and so had an interest in preventing raw wool from reaching his foreign competitors, obtained the necessary warrants to arrest the men involved. In one of his early ventures in 1669 he seized the captain of a ship at Dover, but was forced to allow his prisoner to escape when the women of Folkestone hurled stones at him. He was more successful during the 1680s, seizing twenty French and ten English ships involved in the trade. His most famous exploit took place in 1688 after he had arrested a group of owlers on Romney Marsh. Carter took them before the Mayor of Romney, who granted the smugglers bail. The same night Carter and his men made a further attempt to stop wool being shipped, but were attacked as they rode through Lydd. An ugly situation was developing, and the Mayor's son advised Carter to leave Lydd early next morning and take refuge at Rye. Though Carter accepted this advice, his party was chased by fifty armed horsemen as they rode past Camber to Guldeford Ferry. Here they were rescued in the nick of time by boats from other vessels anchored in the harbour.

The government finally took action in 1698. Riding Officers were appointed under Henry Baker (Surveyor General for Kent), who were to enforce the controls imposed, with the help of mounted troops. It was forbidden for anyone living within 15 miles of the coast to buy wool, and farmers within 10 miles of the sea had to account for their fleeces within three days of a shearing. There were all manner of ways to evade these controls, but, for a time at least, owling was reduced. In 1703 Henry Baker was sufficiently confident to recommend that the number of Riding Officers could be reduced to save money. He was soon proved wrong. When Daniel Defoe rode through Hythe towards Rye in the 1720s he saw Riding Officers and dragoons searching the marshes for wool smugglers '... as if they were huntsmen beating up their game...' Though the officers sometimes scored successes, they were usually so outnumbered that they could only stand and watch as the wool was carried on board ship straight from the horses' backs, and taken immediately to France.

At this point we need to take up the story of the Mayfield gang and its leader. Gabriel Tomkins had been a humble bricklayer from Tunbridge Wells, but must have been a highly intelligent and capable organiser. He became gang leader well before 1717, and his men were known to be successful owlers and Jacobite sympathisers. Ten leading members were farmers and regarded as men of substance. They made frequent forays to the coast in parties of 20 or 30, well armed and riding in open defiance of the law, to load the wool onto waiting French vessels. Brandy, silks and other goods were brought back in a profitable two-way trade. The gang often used the beaches near Lydd and Fairlight, but from 1717 to 1721 they were also running goods near Hastings, Eastbourne and Seaford. Though ruthless, they were not wantonly cruel, and when faced with opposition preferred to tie up or disarm their opponents, and free them once the run was completed.

In 1717 Gabriel Tomkins was indicted for the murder of Riding Officer Gerard Reeves during an affray at Langney Bridge near Eastbourne, but he was subsequently acquitted. In January 1721 he was involved, with other gang members, in a struggle with Excisemen at the Swan Inn at Reigate and another episode at Bletchingly nearby. Two months later, Jacob Walter and Thomas Bigg (two other important gang members) came ashore from a French vessel near Dungeness Lighthouse, and were seized and taken in chains to the George Inn at Lydd. While they were being held in an upper room there in the charge of six armed officers, nine other smugglers burst in, raced upstairs firing their guns, and in the ensuing confusion, succeeded in freeing Walter and Bigg. Gabriel Tomkins, who was evidently one of the rescue party, was shot in the arm. In September 1721 Tomkins, along with other gang members, was intercepted near Burwash, pursued and finally captured in a lane at Nutley on Ash-

Goudhurst Church, where the Goudhurst Militia defeated Thomas Kingsmill and the Hawkhurst gang, April 20th 1747.

down Forest. The capture of Gabriel Tomkins effectively broke up the
Mayfield gang, though his brother and other gang members con-
tinued operations from the Horsham and West Chiltington areas of
West Sussex. Gabriel Tomkins himself was soon to reappear in east
Kent, but in a very different role.

The only tangible reminders of the owling trade in today's landscape are several inns. Two with smuggling connections are the
Woolpack, just off the A259 near Brookland, and another Woolpack
Inn at the charming hamlet of Warehorne, four miles further north.
The latter was linked by a tunnel to the church. (Though this is now
blocked up, it is still periodically inspected by the Excise!) Another
legacy from the owling period was the public support for the smugglers at all levels of society, including many of those charged with the
maintenance of law and order. Typical instances during the 1730s
include an occasion when the Mayor of Winchelsea and Supervisor of
Riding Officers discharged a prisoner accused of assaulting one of his
own men, and the revelation that dragoons based at Lydd and
Romney frequently sold their seizures to an Exciseman at the
remarkable rate of a guinea a horse and 2/- for a half anker of brandy!
Poor Captain Pigram, Commander of the Revenue vessel based at
Rye, explained that he dare not leave harbour without the protection 69

of a man-of-war, because three large Calais sloops loaded with brandy were waiting just outside. Even inside the harbour his small vessel was not immune from attack. On one occasion when smugglers boarded her, several crew members were wounded, and one lost his wig and trousers in the fight!

However, we must return to the career of Gabriel Tomkins. Following his capture in 1721 he was sentenced to seven years transportation, but proceeded to give the authorities such valuable information that he was soon at liberty again. During 1728 he and Jacob Walter were vigorously pursuing their trade, each with a price of £100 on his head, and the following year they were involved in a skirmish at Battle, after landing what was said to be vast quantities of brandy. Back in prison once more, Gabriel Tomkins gave copious information, and was asked to testify before Sir John Cope's official inquiry into abuses in the Customs service. Though he managed to avoid betraying his associates, Tomkins explained in detail how he operated, and claimed to have sold between 15,000 and 20,000 lbs of tea and coffee to London dealers in a year. His cooperation convinced the authorities of his change of heart, and he was appointed a Riding Officer! John Collier remained suspicious of his activities, and was warned by an informer that Tomkins continued to be a double-dyed villain. However, by 1735 he was a Custom House Officer at Dartford, and Bailiff to the Sheriff of Sussex! It was in this last capacity that he was sent to Rye to arrest a smuggler called Moore, and stayed at the Mermaid Inn. The local magistrate released Moore on bail, as so often happened. Moore later went back to talk to Gabriel Tomkins, apparently in the belief that he would be able to buy the incriminating documents. When this failed, a group of local smugglers, helped by the landlord, dragged Tomkins from his room, seized his official papers, and put him on board a vessel in the harbour in order to take him to France. (Considering his record it is remarkable that they did not murder him on the spot!) Only the prompt action of the commander of the Revenue sloop secured his release.

Gabriel Tomkins' later career was also full of incident. He managed to retain his post at Dartford until 1741, when he was forced to make a moonlight flit and disappear. Five years later the Board of Customs notified its officers that Gabriel Tomkins was wanted for robbing the Chester Mail Coach (he is described as being marked by smallpox). He was also implicated in documents seized in 1747 during a smuggling run by Hawkhurst men at Reculver. Then, using the alias Joseph Rawlins, he took part with Hawkhurst men in a robbery at Selbourne in Hampshire. Justice finally caught up with him in 1750; he was tried at Bedford Assize for robbing the Chester Mail and was duly hanged.

The Mermaid Inn at Rye, once frequented by the Hawkhurst gang, and where Gabriel Tomkins was seized by smugglers.

Well before the final disappearance of Gabriel Tomkins, it was clear that both the Groombridge and Hawkhurst gangs were also operating on Romney Marsh, although they more usually landed their goods between Hastings and Pevensey. The first incident in which the Groombridge gang are known to have taken part began on the edge of Romney Marsh in 1733. Officers from both Rye and Hastings dared to search out a gang of 30 armed men with 50 horses who had been seen heading inland through Iden, north of Rye. The officers caught up with the smuggling convoy at Stonecrouch (on the A21 a mile beyond Flimwell), but were disarmed and threatened with pistols ready cocked and held to their heads. They were forced to walk with the party for the next five miles on the road towards the smugglers' headquarters at Groombridge. They were finally released near Lamberhurst and given back their weapons (now unserviceable), and later reported that the leaders called themselves Old Joll, Toll, The Miller, Yorkshire George, Nasty Face and Towzer. (We know Towzer was Isaac Pope from Groombridge.) Three years later, when the same gang was landing tea at Fairlight, William Weston from Rotherfield and John Bowra from Groombridge were captured. Bowra was later acquitted, and William Weston escaped through a   71 window, using a rope his wife had brought concealed in her pocket! The leading members of the Groombridge gang were to remain at large until justice finally caught up with them at Rochester in 1749. It was then that Jerome Knapp (presumably a former gang member) revealed the names of those who had landed 3000 lbs of tea at Lydd in 1745.

John Collier, as Surveyor-General of Riding Officers for Kent, wrote with increasing concern about the violence and defiance shown by the smugglers. Irish seamen had been involved in the trade for some time, but in 1736 Collier reported that there was a gang of about twenty Irishmen 'lurking about in the woods near the sea coast' at Folkestone. They were smuggling tea there, and had managed to recapture a load held in Folkestone Custom House. The same month Collier had been told by an informer, Thomas Pettit, about another landing at Fairlight Beach, and it was the same informer who had earlier witnessed a battle at Hollington (just inland from Hastings) in October 1735, where for the first time there is a reference to what Pettit called the 'Holkhourst genge'. On that occasion Thomas Carswell and other Custom House officers and regular soldiers had taken up positions on either side of the road and waited to ambush a smuggling convoy. In the fight which followed, the gang managed to

Deal seafront today: it was here in 1784 that William Pitt ordered the destruction of every vessel drawn up on the beach.

escape with their laden horses, but Thomas Peen, a carpenter from Hawkhurst, had been shot by two soldiers. (It is in keeping with contemporary attitudes that the two soldiers were indicted for murder, though we do not know their ultimate fate.)

The next encounter involving the Hawkhurst gang took place in 1740 near Hurst Green and only two miles from Hawkhurst. Thomas Carswell was again involved, with other officers and soldiers. According to John Boxall or Boxwell (a gang member who later informed against his colleagues), about 15 cwt of tea had been landed between Hastings and Bulverhythe and taken to a barn at Etchingham for concealment, while the smugglers refreshed themselves and went to bed. Thomas Carswell and his party found the tea and began to escort it back to Hastings in a waggon. This news reached James Stanford (otherwise Trip, and one of the Hawkhurst gang) and he immediately rode round the neighbourhood collecting as many fellow members as he could. He assembled about thirty men, with their horses and weapons (an eyewitness later supplied the names of about half of these). At Hurst Green they stripped to their shirts for action, drank brandy and swore damnation on anyone who left before the tea had been recaptured. They caught up with the waggon and its escort at the top of Silver Hill (to this day an awkward descent on the main road down to Robertsbridge). Here an exchange of fire left Thomas Carswell dead and a dragoon seriously injured. The smugglers not only recaptured their tea, but they took the dragoons prisoner. The gang then carefully weighed out each man's share of the tea, giving ½ cwt to one who had only arrived in time to assist in the unloading! Among those who were later named as having taken part in this episode was Robert Moreton, presumably the same smuggler who was the recognised leader of the Groombridge gang; there were other occasions later when men from both organisations worked together.

It is known that by 1740 the Hawkhurst gang was fully established under the leadership of Arthur Gray and his brother William, and each was reported as having accumulated great wealth. Arthur Gray built a house, complete with his own bonded store, at Seacox Heath (just west of Hawkhurst), and William had bought a house in Goudhurst. Other leading members were Thomas Kingsmill and his brother George, both of Goudhurst, William Fairall from Horsemonden, and James Stanford, also reported to be very wealthy. At this point Jeremiah Curtis (otherwise Alexander Pollard) enters the picture. One report claims that Curtis was a natural son of one of the Lambs, the leading family in Rye. He had organised his own gang, known as the Transports, and had apparently been working with another group led by John Grayling in the Hastings area. In May 1742 'the Curtis Lot' were held responsible for terrorising two of 73

Collier's officers, John Darby and Freebody Dray. The two officers had been attempting to seize a load of brandy when they were intercepted by smugglers who took both them and the brandy towards Dungeness Point, where a gang of fifteen or sixteen were loading tea onto horses. The gang then put the two officers on board the smuggling vessel. They were carried over to Boulogne where (in the event) they were well treated and soon returned to Kent. Their horses were sent to meet them at the George Inn at Rye, so one can only assume that the intention was to frighten and not to harm the officers. Poor John Darby was to be repeatedly threatened, and at one point he and his family were driven from their home at Lydd, and had to take refuge in Hythe. Just when Jeremiah Curtis merged his private army with the much larger Hawkhurst gang is unclear. Certainly he later became one of its most ruthless members, and was to outlive most of them!

During the 1740s the Hawkhurst men under Arthur Gray carried out a whole series of acts of violence. They are known to have sat drinking in the Mermaid Inn at Rye, with their weapons on the table before them, but it was when twenty of them visited the Red Lion nearby that they deliberately frightened the local people by firing in the air. James Marshall, a young bystander who showed unwise curiosity in their affairs, was taken away and never heard of again.

Two major attacks occurred in 1746 and 1747. The first concerned the landing of a huge cargo of tea (a report says 11½ tons!) in Sandwich Bay, which was to have been collected by a joint force of Hawkhurst men and a local gang from Wingham. Something went wrong, and the Wingham group left with their loads before the landing was successfully completed. Whereupon, the Hawkhurst men, furious at losing part of the cargo, collected their weapons and returned to teach a lesson to their unsatisfactory collaborators. They fought with swords, wounding seven Wingham men, and taking back with them forty horses seized from the losers. The second attack was on Goudhurst, and is the more famous. By 1747 local opposition to the terror tactics of the gang was mounting, and the people of Goudhurst began to organise resistance. Under 'General' George Sturt (a former soldier) they set up the Goudhurst Band of Militia and began training. Hawkhurst smuggler Thomas Kingsmill, who was a native of Goudhurst, was infuriated by this development, and sent a challenge to the village. He boasted that on April 20th 1747 he would attack Goudhurst, kill the residents and burn the place to the ground. Rather than submit, the people of Goudhurst organised themselves, dug trenches, collected arms, melted lead for bullets, set up observers' posts and trained under George Sturt to the point where they could fight back effectively. So when Thomas Kingsmill advanced against them on that April day, it was the smugglers who were defeated. Kingsmill's brother George was killed in the first volley, and two more smugglers were to die in later fighting before the Hawkhurst men withdrew.

What is less well known is that at Cranbrook nearby a similar local defence force, called the Cranbrook Association, was formed. This group was responsible for capturing William Potter, a Benenden smuggler, later imprisoned at Maidstone. Then in October 1747 they captured William Gray, but he was released from Newgate on the grounds that he had not been named in the London Gazette as a smuggler, although everyone knew his record. Arthur Gray, meanwhile, was arrested for highway robbery, so the leadership of the Hawkhurst gang devolved on Thomas Kingsmill.

The Hawkhurst gang was not the only one responsible for a spate of violent incidents throughout the whole length of the east Kent coast during the mid 1740s. Secure in their superiority of numbers and weapons, the smugglers cursed and assaulted officers and landed their goods in broad daylight without serious interference. The authorities knew that as much as five tons of tea might be hidden in Brockman's Barn near Folkestone, and they received four reports in ten weeks about goods run at Dymchurch Wall, but could do little to prevent it. When a smuggling cutter and its load of tea was being held

Dymchurch Wall, the scene of innumerable smuggling runs. Part of this coastal defence is thought to date from Roman times.

75

in Dover harbour, two hundred men with cocked pistols rode through the town to recover the vessel. Another gang, not content with making a successful landing on a favourite beach between Hythe and Sandgate, returned a few days later to attack the officer on duty in Sandgate Castle. Finally in 1749 there began the series of trials and executions which broke up the major gangs, and relative peace descended on the Wealden and coastal villages of Kent for a generation.

Smuggling was already increasing again, in response to higher Customs duties, by the time John Wesley first visited Rye in 1758, and he was to preach constantly against the practice. A shadow was cast over his later visits by the failure of this campaign, and still more when his daughter's fiancé, Captain Henry Haddock who commanded the Rye Revenue vessel, was shot by a smuggler off Dungeness. When the whole country was denuded of fighting men during the War of American Independence which began in 1775, the way was open for defiant gangs to operate once more, particularly at Deal, Folkestone and Sandgate. One of the richest seizures ever made took place in 1773, when silk and lace worth £15,000 was captured near Hythe, but it was the seamen of Deal who caused the greatest problems. Deal boatyards had perfected the building of open galleys, often called 'centipedes', up to seventy feet long, with twenty oarsmen and a small sail. It was said one could reach the French coast in two hours. The local seamen regularly brought back goods from shipping in The Downs (including vessels in quarantine), and the government decided that firm action was necessary. In October 1781 over a hundred cavalry and nine companies of infantry were sent to ransack the town for contraband. A timely hint had enabled the townsmen to ship back the bulk of this across the Channel, so the amount seized was said to be worth a mere £10,000 or £15,000 instead of the £100,000 worth which had previously been stored there. But then in January 1784, when the local boats were beached to avoid the winter storms, William Pitt again took action, and sent a regiment of soldiers and an offshore force of naval cutters. The men of Deal watched what they believed was a military exercise, and discovered too late that their boats were to be burned. It was terrible retribution, but it did not stop the smuggling traffic.

In common with seamen at Folkestone and elsewhere in Kent, men from Deal developed a lucrative trade carrying gold guineas across to France by galley during the Napoleonic Wars. They also continued to bring goods ashore in the more traditional fashion. In December 1801, when two revenue vessels had driven a smuggling lugger onshore near Deal, the crew jumped overboard and went to seek local help. Then while the Revenue men were struggling to refloat their

East Wear Bay and The Warren, behind Folkestone; a notorious landing site. Gold guineas were rowed to France from this beach during the Napoleonic Wars.

prize, they were set upon by a horde of armed residents! Beside tobacco, the lugger had been carrying fashionable fabrics and playing cards, and it is noticeable that luxury items figured among the goods carried at this time. A king's messenger was arrested for bringing in silk kerchiefs, and an Excise officer found 4000 yards of French lace and 246 pairs of gloves in a post chaise leaving Deal.

Further down the coast at Sandgate the chief problem was an illicit tobacco factory operating in buildings close to the castle. Despite the establishment of a Watch House in the castle itself, there were regular landings along this beach. In 1786 when two Riding Officers and dragoons had successfully captured some tobacco, the preventive men had themselves to be rescued from the wrath of the local population through the intervention of the Mayor of Folkestone. Three years later officers, supported by a constable and armed with the appropriate search warrant, tried again to gain entry to the tobacco factory, but were driven off ignominiously. There was even a revival of the owling trade. In 1787 smugglers were imprisoned in Dover for attempting to ship live sheep to France from Dymchurch, but in characteristic fashion they were able to escape with outside help and an 'iron crow'. Huge quantities of wool were seized in Romney Marsh 77 before these could be shipped, and were then sold at Rye. At a single sale in 1778 nearly 8000 lbs of wool were on offer.

In 1792 England was again at war with France, and fighting continued until the final defeat of Napoleon at Waterloo in 1815. The fighting did not necessarily prevent smuggling, and Napoleon had good reason to encourage it, but the concentration of troops along the Kent coast, the activities of the press gang and preparations designed to resist invasion certainly made it more difficult. In 1803, after 2650 tubs of gin had been landed near Dungeness in circumstances which threw doubt on the loyalty of the Waterguard, the Collector of Customs at Dover reported to his superiors that smuggling at Deal and Folkestone was greater than ever. However, the smuggling community now had to contend with Watch Houses at key points, and the men of the Waterguard offshore, improved fortifications at Dover, the barracks at Deal and the new Shorncliffe Camp behind Sandgate. In 1795 a chain of signal stations linked to London was established along the coast. Potentially the greatest threat to the smugglers came when the building of a chain of Martello Towers began in 1805, and the Royal Military Canal and Military Road cut Romney Marsh off from its hinterland in 1806. To complete their discomfiture, galleys suitable for taking gold to France were to be destroyed under legislation of 1812. For a time at least smuggling languished.

Following the victory at Waterloo, and almost as soon as the former fighting men returned to restart the smuggling trade, Captain McCulloch (Flogging Joey to his men) put forward the idea of a Coast Blockade to protect the most notorious coasts. In 1817 this was tried out between Margate and Dover and soon extended to cover all shores from Sheerness to Seaford in Sussex. McCulloch organised it from his headquarters on a Man-of-War off Deal. Parties of naval seamen patrolled offshore, and manned the Watch Houses which were sited at intervals of three or four miles (several remain; the one at Old Stairs Bay near Walmer is now a private house). It was McCulloch's boast that he would make grass grow in the streets of Deal! Though the system was both expensive and unpopular, and some blockade men succumbed to bribery, the impact on smuggling was considerable, and was to continue until the Coastguard service took over here in 1831.

But if circumstances had changed, public attitudes had not. The free traders could still count on popular support, as when the crew of a smuggling vessel (who came from Folkestone and Sandgate) were caught in 1820 and imprisoned in Dover gaol. Local people discovered exactly where they were being held, and a strong band of citizens attacked the gaol, got on the roof and began to demolish the place.

They succeeded in rescuing the seamen (while the Mayor of Dover tried unsuccessfully to read the Riot Act) and carried them off to hiding, pausing briefly at the Red Cow in Dover for their manacles to be struck off.

Local seamen continued to own and crew the smuggling vessels. The large galleys which had been used for the gold smuggling trade were now replaced by smaller, cheaply-built open boats, known as 'cocktails'. Men rowed out to pick up rafts of tubs which had been left in mid Channel, but this technique soon fell victim to the Coast Blockade. Guile and deceit worked better. A very good example was later recalled by William Wills, otherwise Yan Yenner, who was born in 1800. He went to sea as a fisherman at thirteen, and became a smuggler at twenty because it paid better. After various successful runs to Ireland, he was among the crew of the *Four Brothers* (owned by his uncle and captained by his father) which left Flushing for Ireland in January 1823 with a cargo worth £11,000. The Revenue cutter *Badger* caught them at daybreak off Dieppe. Unable to escape, the *Four Brothers* hoisted Dutch colours and opened fire. They were forced to surrender, and were later tried at Bow Street, but were acquitted on the bogus grounds that the vessel and more than half the crew were

Sandgate Castle (built by Henry VIII) was used as a preventive Watch House; the beach was regularly used especially in the 1780s, when tobacco was manufactured in buildings close by.

79

The Bourne Tap, the unlicenced beerhouse built by George Ransley, leader of the last Kent gang.

Dutch. To add insult to injury, the *Badger* cutter had to escort the *Four Brothers* out of Dover harbour.

Other seamen came to rely on vessels with specially devised hiding places, many of which were built at Rye. The most famous was the *Sally*, of Hastings, which was constructed as a boat within a boat, leaving a five inch gap between her inner and outer shells for the carrying of contraband. Concealment on land was also becoming more ingenious. Blockademen found one of the cleverly contrived hides in Sandwich Bay in 1817. Tubs had been hidden in a deep wood-lined pit, with a thick layer of shingle on top to defeat its discovery by probing.

The land smugglers also returned to their old techniques and were soon involved in serious fighting with the Blockademen. Contemporary newspaper reports and the recollections of those who took part provide a wealth of detail about episodes in the 1820s right along the coast. One revealing account concerns two Customs men who in 1819 agreed to avert their eyes (in return for a handsome gift of spirits) when smugglers brought a boat into Rye harbour. Unfortunately HMS *Severn* arrived unexpectedly and 'helped' to capture the whole cargo. The aggrieved smugglers thereupon reported the conspiracy, calling as witness their look-out man.

But many stories illustrate the courage of the preventive services. Lieutenant Peat, a Blockademan at Folkestone, showed particular devotion to duty. He had the grim task at Dymchurch of escorting ashore a prisoner called Walker. The local people rioted and threw stones, and in the fight which followed, Peat killed his prisoner. Thereafter he was a marked man. He was twice attacked and ambushed, and on the second occasion survived fourteen wounds. Richard Morgan, a Blockade midshipman at Dover, was later to die for his zealous service. His story is bound up with that of the last Kent gang, the Blues or the Aldington gang.

The first direct reference to this gang came in November 1820, though it must have been responsible for earlier episodes at Deal, St Margaret's Bay and on the marsh. It was led by Cephas Quested until his capture in 1821, and thereafter by George Ransley. We know many details about the gang because Lord Teignmouth (Henry Shore) later talked both to George Ransley's son and to one of his tub carriers. More recently John Douch has taken the story further, with help from Mr Terry Ransley.

In November 1820 the Aldington gang carried out a landing in the traditional style close to Sandgate Castle. Three hundred men were involved, and armed guards protected each flank of the convoy right from the beach and up the Military Road leading inland. They were challenged by local Blockademen and others coming off duty at nearby Martello Tower 4, but the main preventive force had been lured elsewhere. One smuggler was recognised, but none were captured; they left behind their boat and part of their cargo. Moreover, the servant of a gentleman visiting Sandgate was confronted by a wounded man with a blackened face seeking help! The following February a battle took place outside Brookland which left five men dead and twenty five injured, the most savage encounter in the smuggling records. Some 250 men had gone down to the coast east of Camber. A third had been detailed to fight if necessary, while the rest carried the cargo. They were spotted, and a party came from Camber Watch House. A running battle developed across Walland Marsh in which one preventiveman and four smugglers died. In the confusion and darkness, gang leader Quested mistakenly ordered one of the Blockademen to fire on an officer. He was captured and subsequently tried and hanged (but without betraying his colleagues). The wounded were treated by Dr Ralph Hougham, who lived in Pear Tree House, which still stands in the main street of Brookland. He had become accustomed to treating both sides in these struggles, and had a special wallet containing medicines and instruments for use on these occasions. He was also used to being blindfolded and led on his own horse to treat an injured smuggler.

The Watch House of the Coast Blockade at Rye Harbour, which commanded what was then the shoreline.

After the Battle of Brookland George Ransley took over as gang leader. He was born at Ruckinge in 1782, and spent his early life blamelessly as a carter and ploughman. It is said that soon after his marriage he found a cache of spirits, and raised enough money from its sale to build his own house. Known as the Bourne Tap, this can still be seen. Ransley now turned to smuggling. According to his son, he used to go to France by packet boat to buy supplies (200 tubs of spirit was a normal load). Folkestone men in his pay would bring the cargo over, to be met by a well-organised and locally-recruited landing party. He could sell up to a hundred tubs a week from his house, and his customers came from thirty or forty miles around! He retained his own firm of solicitors and a resident surgeon against eventualities!

Under Ransley's leadership the gang continued to land cargoes at points between Deal and Rye. In May 1826, when a galley trying to evade pursuit ran aground at the mouth of the Rother, two hundred men emerged from behind Camber sand hills to stop interference from those at Camber Watch House. The smugglers killed a Blockademen, but then fled, taking their wounded with them. (Camber Watch House, now a private residence, is the last house on the road from Camber towards Lydd.)

The fate of the gang was finally sealed in July 1826 when they were caught unloading tubs onto the beach at Dover (where Marine Parade now stands). Midshipman Richard Morgan from HMS *Ramillies* had come off duty from the Blockade station at Townend Battery about 1 a.m. when he heard men calling to one another on the beach. He fired a shot to summon assistance, but in the ensuing battle among the bathing huts, he was fatally wounded. No one came forward to claim the £500 reward which was offered for information. However, two other gang members who had been captured in earlier fighting now provided the necessary evidence. Ten weeks later Bow Street Runners and Blockade officers went to Aldington at 3 a.m. and surprised the gang leaders in their beds. They were duly tried, but since darkness had made it difficult to identify Morgan's killer with certainty, the death sentences passed were commuted to transportation for life. George Ransley became a convict labourer on a free settler's farm in Tasmania. He was eventually pardoned, became a free settler himself, and seems to have ended his days there with the rest of his large family.

The breakup of the Aldington gang effectively ended large scale smuggling in east Kent. Following a landing at Jury's Gut in 1829, the last convoy went openly through the middle of Lydd while the local people cheered! Desultory efforts continued, particularly south of Rye, where Toot Rock in Pett Level was a recognised meeting place. On one occasion several smugglers were drowned in the Royal Military Canal near Pett, when they failed to find the recognised fording place. A fiddler from Winchelsea was the last man to be killed in east Kent in a smuggling affray near Camber Castle in 1838. However, the stories of what had taken place lived on. The Rev. R H Barham, who ministered to the joint marsh parishes of Snargate and Warehorne, wrote the poem about smuggling which appeared in *The Ingoldsby Legends*. He regularly met smugglers on his journeys through the marsh, and claimed that he could find Snargate church on a dark night by the smell of tobacco stored in its tower. (Virtually all the marsh churches were used in this way, and a vault under the nave at Ivychurch was especially useful.) The story of the Aldington Gang was the inspiration behind G P R James' novel *The Smugglers* and Russell Thorndike's series of stories on the adventures of Dr Syn. It is entirely in keeping with tradition that the sea washed up a dog kennel holding thirty pounds of tobacco at Dungeness in 1843, and bales of leaf tobacco near Sandgate in 1877! The men of Deal kept going even longer, and tobacco, brandy and gin were still being seized by Coastguards during the 1880s.

Dover about 1830. Richard Morgan was murdered by smugglers on this beach in July 1826.

PLACES TO VISIT

Two walks

St Margaret's Bay to Old Stairs Bay, Walmer and Deal. (5 miles)
Parking beside the memorial above St Margaret's Bay at TR 373452. Approach along the B2058, turning left at the crest of the final descent to the bay along Granville Road; keep straight on to the memorial. The walk north from here is along the Saxon Shore Way (a specially signed long distance footpath between Rye and Gravesend). The path follows the cliff edge over downland preserved by the National Trust, and gives startling views of wrecks on the Goodwin Sands on a clear day. Presently all the smuggling beaches at Walmer, Deal and Sandwich Bay come into view. Beside the steps at Old Stairs Bay are the Victorian Coastguard cottages and the Old Watch House, the Coast Blockade station which preceded them. The route continues along Undercliff Road, turning right at the Rising Sun Inn, and left along the unmade road parallel to the shore. At Walmer the beach was one of the battlegrounds of the Aldington gang in 1826. Walmer Castle is the official residence of the Lord Warden of the Cinque Ports. Here a

84

smuggler brought news of the victory at Camperdown in 1797 to William Pitt, and here too Wellington died. On the beach in Deal itself, the six oared galley punt *Undaunted* is preserved by the pier (a reminder of the January day in 1785 when Pitt had all the boats destroyed). The seamen and smugglers lived in the small houses of Middle Street and other narrow alleys nearby, which are now a Conservation Area. The Museum of Maritime and Local History in St George's Road is open afternoons during the main season. Here the galley *Saxon King* is preserved, with pictures of how it was rigged, and a model of a smuggling vessel with tubs hung ready for sinking.

Folkestone Warren to Folkestone Harbour. (1½ miles)
The best start is a bus to the Valiant Sailor Inn, on the North Downs crest above Folkestone; the walk is then all down hill! Notice the public bridleway on the north side of the A20, opposite the Valiant Sailor. This was the route the smugglers used to a cache at Hockley Sole farm (TR 245401), now a private house. A signed footpath beside the inn heads south, straight for the cliff edge, with a remarkable view over East Wear Bay, Folkestone and the distant French coast. The contraband was landed on the sands of East Wear Bay and brought up to the notorious Warren House, which stood just south east of Martello 1 (landslides and the building of the railway have altered some features since). It was then carried up the path to the Valiant Sailor Inn, and sheep were driven after the convoy to obscure the traces. Continue down the smugglers' route past the Martello Towers (the first three of 74, built between 1805 and 1812 against the threat of invasion from France). The beach at Copt Point was formerly more extensive. It was from here that the galleys were rowed over to France, the oarsmen swathed in special purses stuffed with gold guineas. A careless smuggler once left behind a considerable haul on the beach! The route descends past East Cliff Pavilion and down steps to the promenade which leads round to the Stade, the old landing place. (Thomas Telford designed the first harbour here in 1808, but the large western pier was added when the railway came in 1843.) The fishermens' quarter and smugglers' houses, with cellars and escape tunnels, lay behind the Stade. Only old street names such as The Durlocks and Old Radnor Street survive as reminders of the time in the 1740s when, according to Admiral Vernon, there were 300 smugglers living here.

The steep and cobbled High Street above Folkestone Harbour is a surviving remnant of the old town. At one stage 3½ gallon casks of spirit stolen from the Custom warehouse were sold for 10/- at the Folkestone Arms Inn! Turner was one of many distinguished   85 nineteenth century visitors to Folkestone. He was fascinated by what took place offshore, and painted several scenes which featured the Folkestone smugglers at work.

View Points and Other Visits

Goudhurst

Public parking south east of village centre. A delightful Wealden village on a hilltop, the site of the famous battle between the Hawk-hurst gang led by Thomas Kingsmill, and the Goudhurst Band of Militia under George Sturt, on April 20th 1747. St Mary's church has a commanding position, and there was a tunnel from the church to the Star and Eagle Inn at the top of the main street. Spyways, another old house with smuggling associations, stands further down the hill.

Aldington

A scattered and unremarkable village above Romney Marsh, but with several points of interest. The Bourne Tap, the house George Ransley built, and from which he sold spirits, stands beside a minor road at TR 047364, and has now been extended as a private house. He once worked as a carter at Court Lodge Farm (TR 076363). The Walnut Tree Inn in the village centre, was one of a number his gang patronised. Aldington Knoll was their lookout over the marshes (parking on the B2067 at TR 072354).

Dymchurch

Public parking on the A259. The Ship Inn, famous for its associations with smuggling and Russell Thorndike's mythical hero, Dr Syn, has since been enlarged, but still has copies of original documents report-ing what went on, in the bar. Nearby are the church, rectory and manor house, and New Hall, where the bailiffs met to oversee the drainage problems of the marsh. Dymchurch Wall, the ancient defence against the sea and site of innumerable illicit landings, is best seen at high tide. Martello Tower 24 has now been restored and is open to visitors. It was a Coast Blockade station during the 1820s. Herring Hang was another regular landing place, and was between Dymchurch and Hythe.

Lydd

The church, the Town Hall and the George Inn stand in the High Street (which runs along what was once a shingle bank in the wide Rother estuary). All recall former splendours, and it was at the George in 1720 that Jacob Walter and Thomas Bigg were freed by nine other smugglers in a typical armed attack. In the churchyard are buried the victims of the Battle of Brookland and many other fights, and also Francis Sisley, smuggler and grandfather of the French painter. Lydd was the most notorious of all the marsh centres; it was here in 1829 that the inhabitants cheered as a convoy of eighty men and twelve carts passed through after the last major landing.

Rye and Rye Harbour

Public carparks in Rye. Rye must be explored on foot, and preferably out of season. There are many ancient and fascinating buildings, especially the medieval Landgate, St Mary's Church and the Ypres Tower. Those with smuggling associations include the Mermaid Inn, frequented by the Hawkhurst gang, and the Flushing Inn in Market Street, with an early sixteenth century wall painting and cellars which date from before the disastrous French attack of 1377 in which much of Rye was burned. Opposite the Flushing Inn is a bakery where there is still a lift mechanism in the chimney for raising casks to a hiding place in the attic. Above the quay and warehouses on the west side of the old town, Traders Passage linked the notorious London Trader Inn in Mermaid Street with the delightful Watchbell Street and its lookout. Below the Ypres Tower on the east side of the town are the boatyards and the ferryman's house, a reminder that Rye was still virtually an island in 1700.

Rye Harbour, approached from the A259 just west of the town, also deserves a visit. (Parking by Martello 28 at TQ 942188.) A row of buildings here face onto what was the coastline about 1800. A brooding black structure with a lookout window is the Coast Blockade Watch House (the Victorian coastguard cottages which replaced it stand further back, and have now been superseded by a modern building). A short walk along the edge of Rye Bay Nature Reserve takes one to the present shoreline. This gives a very clear idea of the kind of beach which the smugglers regularly used. Across the Rother mouth (scene of various struggles) the fine sands of the shore at Camber and the sand dunes behind were yet another battle ground. 87

(Those interested will find the nature reserve is a bird watchers' paradise; other local features include the sad remains of Smeaton's short-lived harbour protruding through the shingle at Winchelsea beach, and the ruins of Henry VIII's Camber Castle.)

6

The Beaches of Hastings, Bexhill and Eastbourne

The fine beaches of Hastings, Bexhill and Eastbourne, popular with holiday makers and retired residents alike, provided exactly what was needed for landing contraband in quantity two centuries ago. Bearing in mind that most such episodes went unrecorded, it is astonishing how much violent activity took place along this twenty-mile stretch of coast between 1700 and 1840. One of the regular landing sites at Hastings is now at the heart of the town, in front of the Queen's Hotel and Tourist Information Centre; at St Leonards (created by James Burton after 1828) the statue of Queen Victoria in Warrior Square marks a similar spot. At Bexhill the goods were carried up what is now Sea Road to the old village centre by the church, and the last man to die violently in a smuggling affray at Eastbourne was shot between the Wish Tower and Meads Coastguard station in 1833.

In 1700 hardly anyone lived close to the shore except at Hastings itself. Before the groynes were built, the sands were more extensive and continuous, and at low tide the carts and coaches travelled this way in preference to the roads further inland. Hastings itself had a long association with the sea, and had been the head port of the ancient Cinque Ports Confederation. Throughout the smuggling years its extent was no more than the small oval of tightly packed houses and narrow alleys behind the Stade and east of the castle (today's Old Town), although by 1820 the fashionable Marine Parade extended west towards the foot of Castle Hill. The congested centre of the town today (where Queen's Road, Cambridge Road and Robertson Road cross) was the site of the ancient silted-up harbour, occupied in 1820 by boat building yards, a rope walk and a scatter of mean houses which had later to be cleared by Act of Parliament. Some 3½ miles west of Hastings Old Town was Bulverhythe Salts, another early haven as its name implies. Here several streams join to form a small river which struggles through the shingle to the sea. There are still fishing boats beside the river mouth today, and this was

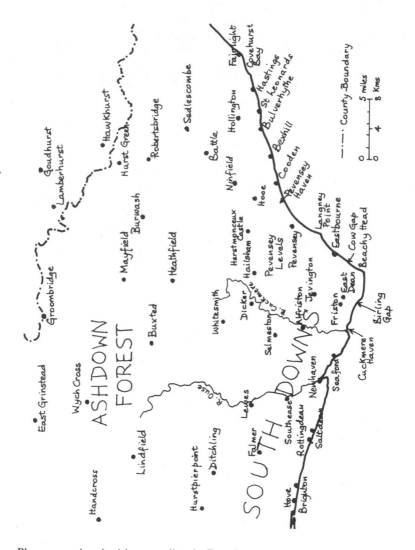

Places associated with smuggling in East Sussex.

Bulverhythe Beach, looking towards Bexhill. Among celebrated landings here was one by the Groombridge gang in 1737, and one in 1828 which led to the Battle of Sidley Green.

perhaps the most notorious of all the landing sites. An alehouse known as Bo Peep stood close to the present West St Leonards Station, and had an unsavoury reputation. These smuggling beaches were well served by a network of roads which ran back along sandstone ridges towards the gang headquarters inland. Eight miles further to the west is Pevensey, where the sea once washed the walls of the Roman fort and later medieval castle. Pevensey was yet another minor Cinque Port whose harbour had been swallowed within the reclaimed marshes of Pevensey Levels before 1700. Though the slow moving waterways here are still known as Pevensey Haven, Hurst Haven and Wallers Haven, the smugglers generally landed their goods on the coast either at Pevensey Sluice (Norman's Bay) or at the Red House (Pevensey Bay), and carried them inland by packhorse. Villages on the fringes of Pevensey Levels (particularly Herstmonceux, Ninfield, Little Common, Hooe and Pevensey itself) were the headquarters of local smuggling gangs. The smuggling beaches continued past Langney and Eastbourne to the fishing and quarrying hamlet of Meads, and Cow Gap below Beachy Head.

Wool from local flocks and cannon from the iron works at Ashburnham were certainly shipped out from here illegally during the seven-

91

teenth century, but the owling trade was relatively unimportant. Instead the records tell of individual Frenchmen coming ashore, following the outbreak of war with France in 1702. Some were probably refugees, but the three men from Calais who landed under Beachy Head in May 1703 were described as having letters and papers, and were probably spies. Five more men were caught here some months later, and others came ashore further west in Sussex. The more typical smuggling enterprises began again with the return of peace in 1712. Three years later, a ship successfully landed brandy at Cowding Gate (Cooden) and then sailed to Cuckmere Haven near Seaford to take on a return cargo of wool, but was intercepted. Thereafter the trade along these shores was increasingly monopolised by the major gangs from inland who came down to collect cargoes of tea.

When in 1717 Riding Officer Reeves was killed at Langney Bridge, on the eastern edge of Eastbourne, the authorities held the Mayfield gang to be responsible. Gabriel Tomkins was indicted for the murder, but subsequently acquitted. His men were certainly using these beaches however. At the charming hilltop village of Mayfield itself, only the cellars of its older buildings and a tall house in Fletching Street provide a link with this violent past.

The 1730s were dominated by the gang based at Groombridge on the county boundary west of Tunbridge Wells. The older houses of Groombridge surround a sloping green, and have that atmosphere of rural charm seen on calendars featuring picturesque Britain. But Groombridge is also just north of Ashdown Forest on the obvious route towards London. The evidence of its villainly is unequivocal; we know the names of the two gang leaders, Robert Moreton and John Bowra. Bowra was wealthy enough to have built himself an impressive house at Groombridge (though we do not know exactly where this was). We know the names of a dozen other gang members (they were awaiting trial in Rochester gaol in 1749). At least eight of these men lived in Groombridge itself, while others came from villages along the routes they commonly used – Rotherfield, Hartfield, Penshurst and Westerham. Throughout the 1730s they rode down to the Sussex coast to collect contraband, normally landed at Lydd, Fairlight, Bulverhythe or the Pevensey beaches, and sold to London dealers. There is some evidence that they sometimes worked with the Hawkhurst men; they certainly operated with the Hooe Company, based at Hooe village above the Pevensey Levels, and James Blackman as landlord of the inn there was an important linkman. The informer calling himself Goring provided much of this detail. He offered to give the names of those taking part in a landing at Bulverhythe in March 1737. The gang had evidently been doing very

Groombridge in Kent, the headquarters of a major gang from about 1730 to 1749.

well. According to Goring, Moreton and Bowra had sold 3000 lbs of tea a week during the winter of 1735/6. The landing in March 1737 was the seventh of that winter, and their only loss in the previous six was ½ cwt 'given to a dragoon and an officer' (as a bribe presumably). However, this particular run had gone wrong. There were twenty-six men involved, including Moreton and his servant Cat; someone said that Thomas Gurr (Stick-in-the-Mud) had fired first. Collison and Pizon (smugglers apparently) had been killed, and they lost half their goods. For all that, another convoy had already left Groombridge for the coast.

Goring also reported that the Hooe Company had lost everything on one occasion, but were soon able to recover from that setback. Much later the Hooe people were among those reported as pillaging the wreck of the Spanish prize, the *Nympha Americana*, wrecked off Birling Gap in 1748. The Groombridge gang also continued to operate until they were betrayed by smuggler Jerome Knapp and held for trial in Rochester in 1749. John Collier described the Groombridge men as an infamous gang which struck terror into the whole countryside. The first time their activities can be identified with certainty was in 1733, when preventive officers were disarmed and forced to accompany their convoy to Lamberhurst. Isaac Pope, known as   93

Towzer, was one of those who took part. His name, with those of John Kitchen (Flushing Jack), Thomas Ward (Bulverhythe Tom), Thomas Gurr and William Weston recur most frequently in episodes at Lydd in 1734, Bexhill, Lydd and Fairlight in 1736, and Pevensey Sluice and Bulverhyhe in 1737. The authorities hit back where they could. William Weston was arrested in 1736 but escaped. Isaac Pope was convicted and sentenced to transportation in 1737, but soon reappeared and was among those caught again in 1749. John Bowra, one of the gang leaders, was arrested in 1737 for running tea between Pevensey and Eastbourne, but it is not clear what then happened; his name does not appear in later records. Robert Moreton continued to lead the gang until their mass arrest in 1749, and this despite the fact that a detachment of soldiers was sent to Groombridge in 1737 to re-establish law and order.

The port of Hastings was more directly involved in sea smuggling during these years. Local men built and crewed the ships which brought in the supplies. However, the gang known as the Hastings Outlaws, or the Transports, led by John Grayling, seems to have operated overland as well. Jeremiah Curtis was one of its members; another was Thomas Holman, who happened to be related to John Collier, then head of the preventive services. Collier therefore found himself in the unhappy position of trying to protect Thomas Holman from the consequences of his involvement in a whole series of criminal activities. As a result of his special pleading, Holman was sentenced to transportation instead of execution, and in fact went to live in France. John Grayling was also sentenced to transportation, but later reappeared in Sussex, and Jeremiah Curtis, indicted at Lewes in 1737, went on to become a leading member of the Hawkhurst gang.

By 1740 it was the men from Hawkhurst who dominated the East Sussex coast as well as Romney Marsh. It was following the landing of tea at Bulverhythe in 1740 and its subsequent capture at Etchingham, that Thomas Carswell was murdered, and men from either Hawkhurst or Groombridge were plainly responsible for three other actions. In June 1744, officers from Eastbourne backed up by dragoons, went to intercept a landing in Pevensey Bay. A hundred smugglers rode up, disarmed and wounded them, and then calmly loaded up their horses and set off for London. Five months later sixty armed men rode up to the home of Riding Officer Philip Bailey at Bexhill, destroyed his household goods and furniture and insulted his wife and family. This was probably to intimidate any opposition to what happened on the next day, when three large cutters landed their goods in Pevensey Bay and (according to the Eastbourne Collector of Customs) carried them inland on 500 or 600 horses. The preventive services were far too weak to provide effective opposition to such tactics. They were forced to rely on informers, and a man called Harrison foolishly became so drunk at an alehouse close to Fairlight church that he fell asleep there, and was very nearly caught by Hastings men infuriated by his actions. One outlawed smuggler was taken while in bed at Hastings, and arrested for having run goods at 'Sea-houses near Eastbourne', the houses which still stand a little east of the pier. However, it was events elsewhere in Sussex which led to the final breakup of the major gangs.

An event of a different kind took place off Bulverhythe in 1748. The *Amsterdam*, outward bound from Holland to Batavia on her maiden voyage, ran aground here. The vessel and her cargo were said to be worth £200,000, and though the silver on board was rescued, she sank into the silt so rapidly that neither the legal salvage men nor the local wreckers had much success. (Partly for this reason the present exploration of the wreck promises to be an important project in marine archaeology.) At the time a Mr Thorpe told John Collier 'The wine is

John Collier's house in Hastings. The letters he wrote here as Surveyor-General of Riding Officers provide the best contemporary account of smuggling in the early eighteenth century.

A seizure at Eastbourne Custom House. This undated print shows tubs being unloaded from a cart labelled 'Birling'. Reproduced by kind permission of the Towner Art Gallery, Eastbourne.

French, if you would have any please let me know. I fancy about a shilling a bottle will be the price.'

The violence and lawlessness already associated with Hastings was confirmed by two cases of piracy, which brought down the government's wrath upon the town. In 1758 a Danish ship carrying the Papal ambassador to Denmark was boarded by two Hastings men who assaulted the master and stole part of the cargo. They were subsequently executed, but worse was to follow. In 1768 a Hastings gang known as Ruxley's Crew (which had already robbed other vessels) boarded a Dutch ship off Beachy Head and killed its master. They were betrayed by their own boasting that they had chopped him down the backbone. In response the government sent a man-of-war and a cutter to convey the guilty men to London, where thirteen were later hanged. Two hundred Inniskilling dragoons were billeted on the town, to the horror of the inhabitants, and one shopkeeper, said to be worth £10,000, fled after being accused of trading with the smugglers.

For many years thereafter things were quieter, but smuggling cutters continued to land goods on all their favourite beaches. Indeed when the Snuin Revenue cutter tried to interfere with one landing under Beachy Head in 1790, the smugglers held the preventivemen captive, and used their ship's boat to run goods ashore. The long years of war with France from 1793 to 1815 brought new problems for the smuggling communities. Signal stations were set up on Beachy Head and at Fairlight, and barracks were built at many points. After 1806 a line of Martello Towers crowned the shoreline, 12 between St Leonards and Cooden (none of which remain) and a further 22 round Pevensey Bay to Eastbourne. Despite this, Napoleon is said to have been regularly supplied with English newspapers from Bexhill. A gang from Little Common, on the edge of Bexhill, began operations from the beach in front of the Star Inn (now Norman's Bay). Smuggling vessels were intercepted here in 1805 and 1806, and one large seizure at Hastings was said to be worth £2800.

The real change came with the return of peace. Hastings was already becoming a fashionable resort, and the creation of St Leonards began in 1828. Bexhill and Eastbourne were still no more than villages, but early visitors lived alongside the smugglers. The son of the proprietress of the bathing machines at Eastbourne was later to be imprisoned for taking part. After 1818 the Coast Blockade took over the preventive role, although some Riding Officers remained. There were two Watch Houses in Hastings itself, and other Blockade patrols were based in the Martello Towers. Contemporary newspaper reports, and the reminiscences of local men make clear that the smugglers now tried bribery, every sort of guile and open warfare by turns, in an attempt to re-establish their profitable activities. As an instance of bribery, in 1819 two men approached the Blockademan in charge of the Martello in Bexhill (near the site of the De La Warr Pavilion). They entertained him at the Bell Inn, and offered him £50 down and a further £50 if he would go at the critical moment to Bulverhythe Point and look the other way! Despite the size of the bribe, he betrayed them. Another Blockademan was effectively 'squared' at the Bull Inn at Bulverhythe.

For seamen the subtle approach included building special compartments into a vessel, and camouflage and muffled oars were used by those who rowed out to creep up tubs left offshore. The well known Hastings smuggler called Roper suffered various misfortunes, despite these precautions. He had already jettisoned one cargo near Littlehampton, but in 1821 was reported to have sailed to Boulogne with four others in a new boat, and was expected to make his next run somewhere near Newhaven. In the event he lost that cargo also. In August 1822 he tried a different idea, and allowed a crew member to act as 'informer' and claim a reward for 'finding' his vessel. The

97

Collector at Newhaven was wise to this game and refused to pay up! Roper also lost his ship *Isis*, condemned for having secret compartments. John Noakes, captain of the *Sally*, seized in 1823, fared rather better. This was a complete boat within the original hull, the intervening space being crammed with contraband. However, since it could not be proved this came from abroad, John Noakes went free, and the Customs were left with the bill for the medical treatment he had required as an epileptic!

Blockademen searched suspicious fishing boats by prodding with a 'pricker', an operation liable to cause damage to the nets. This led to tragedy and a public outcry in March 1821. Joseph Swaine had brought his boat ashore in front of the Stade at Hastings. George England from the Blockade tried to inspect it. Exactly what followed is uncertain because evidence at the Old Bailey trial was conflicting, but an argument developed, and suddenly George England shot and killed fisherman Joseph Swaine. Uproar followed; Swaine may have been innocent, and no one ever searched his boat. He was only 29, and left a widow and five young children. George England was arrested, tried for wilful murder and condemned to death. His pathetic plea that he was only trying to do his duty won him a reprieve, at which the fishermen of Hastings went on strike in fury.

Another tactic was to decoy the preventives away from a landing by lighting a fire in the wrong place or by feeding false information into the system. Philip Kent, who later became a Hastings schoolmaster, remembered with some glee how two of them were arrested while transporting tubs filled with seawater, while the proper cargo was landed unobserved. At this stage the men from Hooe and Herstmonceux rowed out into Pevensey Bay to pick up tubs of brandy and then went round to small gaps in the cliffs further west, at Crowlink or what is now Peacehaven, in hopes of a more secluded landing. One of these four-oared boats, the *Ann* of Pevensey, was caught in 1826. Her master claimed she was fishing, but there was no fishing gear on board; on the contrary the crew were dressed in white, the boat was painted white and she had muffled oars and equipment for creeping up tubs.

The unstable sandstone cliffs between Hastings and Fairlight were now used by men prepared to climb rope ladders and haul up the goods by crane (so-called derricking), but the larger beaches which the owlers had used a century earlier were too closely guarded. (The Haddocks Watch House above Fairlight Cove still stands close to the cliff edge; now a private house, it is the last building one passes on the path from Fairlight towards Cliff End.) As old men, the local smugglers recalled an occasion when they were alerted to the presence of a

The smuggling beaches at Glynde Gap and Bulverhythe; a view towards Hastings from Galley Hill, Bexhill.

sentinel (while cowering on a ledge) by the barking of his dog. There were references to Robin Whiting's Hole, a hide in Ecclesbourne Glen, and to their local meeting place at Dunn's Barn, where Mount Pleasant and Elphinstone roads meet in Hastings now. These cat-and-mouse tactics readily degenerated into violence. When twenty men went down to the shore just east of Fairlight in April 1827, a battle followed in which three smugglers were killed, and the wounded were carried the six miles back to Udimore. Smugglers struggling up the steep and slippery track from Covehurst Bay on a moonlit night in January 1831 were similarly surprised by a Blockade patrol. Two were shot dead in the glen just below Fairlight Place. Clearly these tactics no longer paid.

The more determined smugglers from Bexhill and Little Common were even then relying on superior numbers and brute force. Every attempt was made to intimidate the opposition, and in 1824 the battered body of an overzealous Blockademan was found on Bexhill beach. The most serious fight took place here in the early hours of January 3rd 1828, after a landing near Bulverhythe. Following time-honoured practice, a party of smugglers, protected by some twenty   99

The Star Inn at Norman's Bay. Around 1800 the haven in front of these windows was dominated by the Little Common gang, and it was here that a battle took place in 1822.

others with wooden bats, rushed to bring a cargo ashore. The patrols from Galley Hill station tried to intervene but were outnumbered, and the convoy set off up the road from Glynde Gap towards Sidley (now the A2036). At Sidley Green they were met by forty armed Blockademen, but drew themselves up in military fashion. They fought so furiously that the Blockademen were forced to withdraw, and their leader was killed. An old smuggler called Smithhurst was later also found dead, still clutching his wooden bat. At the Old Bailey trial which followed, ten men were sentenced to death, but later transported. (Some of these men had also been involved in a similar episode at Eastbourne three weeks later.)

More savage battles took place near Pevensey Sluice. In 1822 preventivemen armed with guns had defeated a large gang wielding cudgels and bats outside the Star Inn (close to Norman's Bay Station). But the last and worst battle here took place in November 1833. The landing on the Pevensey Bay shore had been seen by Coastguards, and the unloading was this time carried out under the protection of men who kept up constant gunfire. A running fight developed which lasted for two hours, as the Coastguards chased the smugglers

100

for six or seven miles. By the end, three smugglers were killed and five taken prisoner. None of the Coastguards was injured, and all were later awarded £20 in prize money. The rest of the smugglers escaped across the marsh through the fog, leaving a trail of blood, and heading for Wartling and Boreham Street.

This was effectively the end of major landings which had continued since the days of the Mayfield and Groombridge men. Not surprisingly there is still evidence of specially devised hides that were used for long periods. Pevensey Castle ruins and Herstmonceux Castle (also ruinous after 1780) were certainly used. There is a bricklined tunnel behind the Smugglers' Wheel Restaurant at Boreham Street, and another elaborately constructed concealed entrance to a shaft and tunnel deep underground at the private house called Montague in Hankham, close to Pevensey Haven.

It is appropriate to end this story of the most violent stretch of coastline with one last account of bloodshed. Early on a January morning in 1833 George Pett, in charge of the preventive boat, was talking to a Coastguard on the Eastbourne shore between the Wish Tower and Meads, when a signal from the cliffs was answered by a whistle from the sea. Smugglers rushed down to the beach, protected by armed men on each flank. Although more Coastguards came to help, and there were wounded on both sides, it was George Pett who was killed. No one ever claimed the £1000 offered for information on his assailants.

PLACES TO VISIT

The Smugglers Adventure, St Clements Caves, Hastings
This new museum, on top of the West Hill, near the Castle is reached by numerous footpaths from the Old Town, or via the Lift in George Street (Summer months only), or by car from Priory Road, and a few minutes' walk across the grass. The story of smuggling on the South Coast is brought to life in four acres of sandstone caves. The Caves date back to ancient times, and were almost certainly used by the smugglers of Hastings. Deep in these extraordinary Caves there is an exhibition area, a short audio/visual programme, and as you wander through the caverns and tunnels you will discover life-sized tableaux of the smugglers at work, doing their nefarious deeds. There are murders, a ghost too, plenty of buttons to press and more than a few 'surprises'!

Two Walks
Exploring Hastings Old Town   Start from the Stade, or landing place   101

Herstmonceux Castle; the ruinous shell was used for storage, and the 'phantom drummer' patrolled the first floor corridor of this wing to discourage interference.

behind the beach. Fishing boats still lie here as they did when George England shot Joseph Swaine in 1821. The famous net houses stand nearby, and in the Fishermen's Museum is the lugger *Enterprise*, built in 1909 but essentially similar to vessels the smugglers used. All Saints Street leads past narrow alleys and houses once equipped with secret cupboards and convenient cellars. The Stag Inn can still boast an underground vault from which a tunnel leads up to a cave cut in the sands of East Hill. The oldest house belonged to the mother of Admiral Cloudesley Shovell. Hastings House, the home of John Collier (and later of poet Coventry Patmore) stands above and opposite the church at the apex of Old Town. It was here that he coordinated opposition to the violent gangs of the 1730s and 1740s. Walk back down High Street and George Street, passing a signed footpath to the caves of Castle Hill. These were excavations made by quarrying sand, and were used to store contraband on occasion.

The Cliffs between Hastings and Fairlight Head.   Best starting point is the viewpoint and picnic site on Fairlight Head at TQ 860116, the centre of Hastings Country Park. Approach from Hastings on the minor road between Ore and Fairlight, turning right near Fairlight Church. (Alternative ways in along the cliff path east of Hastings, or from the picnic site at TQ 848117.) Well signed footpaths lead down in all the glens the smugglers used. The shore in Ecclesbourne and Warren Glens can no longer be reached, but Covehurst Bay (Hastings Naturist Beach) is usually accessible unless recent landslips have destroyed the steps. Excellent views of the smuggling beaches along Pett Level and the coast to Dungeness.

Other Visits

Bulverhythe Beach
Best approached from West Marina, St Leonards. This notorious landing place saw some of the worst violence. The wreck of the *Amsterdam* is visible at very low tide.

Boreham Street
The Smugglers' Wheel Restaurant has on display the wheel at the head of a shaft down to the cellars. Recent building work brought to light a bricklined tunnel leading from the cellars towards Wallers Haven, once an arm of the sea, but reclaimed before 1700.

Herstmonceux Castle
The village centre on the A271 is some distance from the church and castle. The castle grounds are open at limited times, but the building itself is not. The moated castle, rebuilt within its 15th century shell, is now part of Greenwich Observatory, and telescopes in the grounds may also be visited. The phantom drummer was reported to walk along the south gallery of the castle (and was the inspiration for Addison's play *The Drummer*). There was also a grey lady, who appeared to discourage visitors. Contraband was stored in the castle ruins and in table tombs beside the church, according to local tradition.

Hooe Village
This scattered village on the B2095 between Pevensey and Ninfield was a smuggling centre for generations. The Red Lion Inn (TQ 692106) dates back five hundred years and is evidently where landlord James Blackman worked with members of the Groombridge gang, and took convoys to Ashdown Forest. Because of his known smuggling exploits, three Jacobites (James Bishop of Parham, his servant and James Ibbotson from near Arundel) sought his help in 1744, when trying to reach France and join the Pretender. It seems he betrayed them, and they were arrested here. The Blackman family continued to live at Hooe (their graves lie beside the isolated village church). In the early 19th century they owned the magnificent Grove 103

Mr Hodgson, landlord of the Hastings Arms at Hastings, with one of the barrels found concealed beneath a window on the first floor. Apparently there were originally six storage barrels under adjoining windows, and the pipes that linked each to the cellar can still be seen. Reproduced by kind permission of Mr Hodgson.

House, just south of the church. Outside the Red Lion today are six lime trees, apparently the local sign for a safe house. In the attic is a contraption for shredding contraband tobacco and making snuff. The Lamb Inn, just off the A259 at TQ 674082 is another ancient hostelry almost certainly involved in the trade.

The Star Inn at Norman's Bay

Approach along the narrow road between Pevensey and Cooden Station. Part of the inn is over five hundred years old, and was the sluice house for men working the sluices on the artificial cut called Wallers Haven. Norman's Bay Station stands more or less on the site of the former haven of Pevensey Sluice, once monopolised by smugglers from Little Common. The last of the violent landings here took place in 1833. A signed footpath beside the inn marks the track regularly used to carry goods towards the Lamb Inn and Hooe village.

7

The Cliffs and Coves from Eastbourne to Brighton

Some of the finest cliffs in southern England line the coast immediately west of Beachy Head. Here the sea has cut into the white chalk, sheering off what were once small valleys and leaving that alternation of tall cliffs and intervening gaps we know as the Seven Sisters. Thanks to the National Trust, enlightened local authorities and the generosity of individual landowners, the seven-mile stretch between Beachy Head and Seaford Head is still undeveloped, and one of the few sections of Channel coast which has remained essentially unaltered since before 1700. A much lower cliff line continues from Newhaven round to Brighton, but here development since 1920 has taken some disastrous forms. Part of the problem is that this coast is exposed to Channel gales (in places the cliff edge is still being lost to the sea at an average rate of a yard a year) and there are no trees to soften the urban sprawl. Throughout the smuggling years activity was inevitably concentrated at the gaps between the chalk ramparts, as much by the naked rock platform revealed at low tide as by the cliffs themselves.

Men from every hamlet and village behind the coast took part in whatever opportunities were available. For centuries they pillaged wrecks or smuggled, though often on a relatively small scale. Only the shingle beaches in the larger bays attracted the major gangs to the area. During the eighteenth century therefore, the records are of landings at Cuckmere Haven, along Seaford Bay and at Saltdean Gap and Rottingdean. After 1817, when the Coast Blockade made things much more difficult, all the smaller gaps were pressed into use, particularly Birling Gap and Crowlink among the Seven Sisters, Hope Gap near Cuckmere, Bearshide (Peacehaven) and Porto Bello (Telscombe Cliffs). The navigable river Ouse was used to carry goods to Lewes or Glynde. Of all the landing places Cuckmere Haven   105

A print of Beachy Head by W S Howitt which shows a landing at Cow Gap near Eastbourne. Reproduced by kind permission of the Towner Art Gallery, Eastbourne.

remains the most evocative. The Blockade Watch House and later Coastguard cottages stand guard over an otherwise empty bay, and one known to have been used by smugglers in this century.

The 'new haven' developed beside the ancient settlement of Meeching was the result of an artificial cut made in 1537 through shingle blocking the Ouse river mouth. Before that the Ouse ran south east-wards, and entered the sea by the ancient (and long decayed) port of Seaford. The harbour at Newhaven was improved during the 1730s and it was from here that the Custom House officers battled to prevent smuggling. Larger vessels were only able to use the port after further improvements around 1825, when HMS *Hyperion* was stationed here to command the western extension of the Coast Blockade.

Contraband landed on this coast could be carried inland along a whole series of drove roads which led over the Downs and through the commons and woods of the southern Weald. Today these are often popular bridleways and paths which run along the crests of ridges. To take one good example, from the west side of Cuckmere Haven the obvious route ran north along the edge of modern Seaford past Chyngton Farm, and curved round to reach the downland crest between Firle Beacon and Bostall Hill. It continued past Bo Peep (a name which recurs at smuggling sites) to Selmeston. There were said

to be depots here, and May's Farm nearby still has extensive cellars.
From here tracks led directly to the large common and fairground site
at Thicket. Just to the west on Laughton Common was Whitesmith
(now on the A22 near East Hoathly), notorious as a haunt of smugglers, and the junction of routes leading on either towards Ashdown
Forest or Mayfield. Partly because the character of both the countryside and the unspoilt villages fit the popular vision of smuggler
country, it is sometimes difficult to disentangle genuine records from
later 'embroidery' about what took place here. Without any doubt
plenty of contraband came ashore on this section of coast; equally
certainly, more was landed elsewhere in Sussex.

The free trade was well established along all the best beaches here
well before 1700. Henry Baker reported in 1698 that the people of
Seaford stored French brandy and wines in their homes and sold these
to retailers in Lewes. Somewhere along the cliffs between Newhaven
and Brighton a smuggler called Garland had vaults where he could
store silk. At times as many as five French sloops would land goods in
a night, and Garland would receive and despatch these valuable
cargoes by the waggon load. The strong link with France was emphas-
ised when Frenchmen, thought to be spies, were caught on the beach
at Seaford in October 1702, and at Newhaven three months later.
Lewes had once been one of the legal ports for the export of wool, and
the owling trade soon followed. In 1714 a French ship which had
brought brandy to Cooden (Bexhill) tried to pick up a return cargo of
wool at Cuckmere Haven, but was captured. The crew (five Frenchmen and an Englishman) were each fined £60, and being unable to
pay, were held in terrible conditions in Horsham gaol for a year.

In the 1720s the Mayfield gang were using the beach at Seaford. It
is generally believed that Edward Tomkins, rather than his brother
Gabriel, was responsible for holding a Customs officer captive while a
cargo was landed, and this was to be the pattern for other landings in
the area in the 1730s. By then the Mayfield gang had broken up, and a
group from Rottingdean were probably responsible for various
attacks. In June 1733 officers from Newhaven were held captive when
they tried to intercept a convoy carrying tea at Cuckmere Haven.
According to W D Cooper, a very similar episode took place two
months later at 'Greenhay' (this is likely to be the place just west of
Rottingdean where the later Blockade and Coastguard stations were
called Greenway). Officers and dragoons did succeed in capturing
five armed smugglers in a major fight near Newhaven the following
year.

In contrast to other parts of the Sussex coast, there is little indication of smuggling during the 1740s, but we know it continued. John
Collier wrote to Henry Pelham at Stanmer House near Brighton   107

A contemporary print which shows wreckers and smugglers pillaging the Spanish prize *Nympha Americana* below Crowlink in November 1747.

about the dangers of carrying large sums of money from 'Thorn' to
Lewes. The list of outlawed smugglers published in November 1748
included six men from the Lewes area: John Clare of Rodmell, Francis
Pollard of Piddinghoe, Samuel Brown and John French of Lewes and
two men from Tarring. (John French was the man captured in
Hastings while in bed feigning illness!) Moreover, in 1749 Thomas
Bassy was gaoled for breaking into the Newhaven Customs warehouse. In the meantime local people had been making the most of two
shipwrecks. In 1747 the English merchant vessel *St Paul* ran aground
at Cuckmere Haven while trying to evade a French privateer.
Accounts of what followed vary, but John Diplock commanding the
Revenue sloop captured her and claimed to be protecting the vessel
against wreckers from Seaford and Alfriston. There is no uncertainty
about what followed the wreck of the *Nympha Americana* near Birling
Gap in November 1747. This Spanish ship had been captured near
Cadiz with an extremely valuable cargo which included mercury.
Various prints exist which show the pillaging of the wreck, and the
Marlipins Museum at Shoreham has an oil painting of the scene, in
which the familiar Seven Sisters coast and Seaford Head are immediately recognisable. Some of the wreckers became incapably drunk
and others died when stolen casks were broached in a cave below the
cliffs. John Collier was told that men from Hooe had 'come in a body
and carried off velvety cloth', which casts an unexpected light on this
gang from the Pevensey Marshes.

This coast remained a constant danger to shipping, and Parson
Jonathan Darby of East Dean enlarged a cave in the cliffs somewhere
below Beachy Head, from which a lantern could be waved on stormy
nights, and which could also be used as a refuge. The first lighthouse
at Belle Tout was not built till 1831, nearly a century later. It is known
that preventivemen patrolling the Seven Sisters cliffs marked the
position of their beat with lumps of chalk, visible at night. It was a
simple matter to move these and lead the unsuspecting patrolman to
fall over the edge (on occasions he may also have been pushed). This
is the explanation traditionally given for the death of Exciseman
Thomas Fletcher in 1750. He lies buried in one of two box tombs just
east of Friston church. Some seventy years later, several Coast Blockade patrols fell to their deaths along this coast; a covering of snow had
made their task particularly dangerous.

The *Sussex Weekly Advertiser* published a number of accounts of
relatively minor smuggling ventures during the 1760s: several cwts of
tea seized at Rottingdean, Newhaven and Beachy Head, for example,
and other cargoes of brandy. An outlawed smuggler called Rowland
was executed at Lewes, and in September 1760 six French prisoners
were seen launching a boat near Saltdean and attempting to escape to

109

France. (This was during the Seven Years War.) At this point William Catt built an important mill worked by tidal power immediately behind one of the favourite beaches between Seaford and Newhaven. A small community grew up beside the tidemill and this remained a regular landing place for the next seventy years. (The houses and mill were severely damaged by the sea in 1876 and later destroyed, though their foundations can still be seen.)

The scale of illegal trading along this coast increased greatly when the War of American Independence left few troops available for preventive duties. After 1793 the long years of war with France exposed the Channel coast to the constant threat of invasion, and raids by French privateers. Substantial seizures of tea and spirits continued, and periodically there were huge sales of seized goods at Newhaven Custom House. Far larger quantities were being landed on the beaches west of Brighton however. For example an official report spoke of three vessels unloading at a time at Shoreham, and the Excise Supervisor at Lewes felt powerless to intervene against the armed convoys as they rode inland. In September 1783 gangs of 200 or 300 men arrived at Cuckmere Haven twice within a week, and

The Coast Blockade Watch House overlooking the smuggling beach at Cuckmere Haven beyond.

defiantly carried off their goods, despite opposition and the fact that
the sea was extremely rough on the earlier occasion. A contemporary
report mentions that it was quite common to see a dozen smuggling vessels lying off the coast in broad daylight at this time. The
authorities were also alerted to what was happening at Tide Mills
when a stormy sea swept a smuggling vessel right over the beach and
into the millpond in 1785. The same year a cutter about to land goods
at Saltdean Gap was chased almost back to the French coast before
being captured. Her cargo was found to be worth £20,000, and
included twelve tons of fine tea and three large bales of lace. The
luxury items and fashionable goods increasingly brought in here were
no doubt intended to satisfy the gentlemen and ladies attending the
Prince Regent at Brighton.

Local communities behind the gaps in the Seven Sisters were doing
very well without attracting undue attention. James Pettit, who used
a variety of other names and is generally known as Jevington Jigg,
kept the inn at Jevington and was the leader of a local gang here in the
1780s. According to Philip Smart's account of his activities, he seems
to have been a determined horse thief as well as a smuggler, and spent
periods in gaol at Battle, Horsham and East Grinstead. By 1792 he
had changed sides and worked for the Excise at 10/- a week (and was
contemptuously known as 'a ten shilling man'). He was working for
Mr Walter of Horsham and helped transport a seizure of tobacco at
Newhaven. He was soon in trouble again for stealing two hams and
hay from a hayrick. Apparently he ended his days in Botany Bay for
horse stealing at Salisbury in 1799. But if Jevington Jigg was no more
than a small time operator, his village was deeply implicated and
figured in various minor episodes. Philip Smart was able to report
that the huge cellars of Jevington Rectory still bore the Exciseman's
mark, but this is no longer visible. A tunnel is reported to have led
from the Eight Bells (a private house in Jigg's day) to Thorpe Cottage, where a trapdoor was closed up in 1956. Another tunnel from
cellars at Filching Manor, the fine medieval house nearby, has now
partially collapsed.

The landing beaches the Jevington smugglers used were at Birling
Gap and below Crowlink (still called Smugglers' Bottom). Before
coastal erosion cut back the cliffs it was still possible for carts to be
taken down to the shore, and the beach at a third gap further west was
also precariously accessible down steps cut in the chalk. Birling Gap
had been sufficiently important at the time of the Armada for orders
to be issued to have it 'rammed up', and Crowlink Gap was protected
by a battery when the *Nympha Americana* was wrecked here in 1747.
Men from East Dean also made profitable use of these beaches; the
evidence is indirect but intriguing. A fine three-storey house known as

111

Dipperays stands just behind the Tiger Inn at East Dean. James Dipperay, who died a rich man in 1791, is reputed to have been a smuggler who turned king's evidence and built the house from the proceeds of his activities. Elizabeth Doff's researches provide a glimpse of the ramifications of the black economy in a small downland village. James Dipperay's relatives were the Willard family who lived at Crowlink, and his nephew inherited Birling Manor nearby. When James Dipperay died, even his gardener (whose name is given as William Worger) benefited from the generosity of his will, and the gardener's youngest son received £1000 and 13 acres of land at Herstmonceux. (All the place names are surely significant!) Thirty years later John West and James Woolgar (could that be Worger?) were the Riding Officers at East Dean. So unsuccessful were they in their chosen profession that an adverse report went to the Board of Customs. The reward for their discretion may be judged by the fact that James Woolgar, on a salary of £60 a year, was presently able to buy his own house and the field which still bears his name!

There is every reason to think that exactly this sort of thing was going on in every village in the area. Rottingdean in particular was deeply implicated in the trade. The Rev Thomas Hooker was vicar there from 1792 to 1838, and certainly took part; it was said that he acted as lookout man for the local gang. The goods were usually landed below Saltdean (which was then empty downland) and carried over the hill by what is now Whiteways Road to the depots in Rottingdean. Bearing in mind that this was a parish of shepherds and farmers, the fine old houses round the Green are indicative of an alternative source of wealth. Hillside, built in 1732, is a good example, and it is claimed that a number of houses have cellars which were linked by tunnels to the shore. The contraband went inland along downland tracks and what is now the road to Falmer (B2123). In 1791 goods were seized in Baldsdean Bottom (north of Saltdean), and four years later casks of spirit were found hidden in a cave at Ovingdean. From the gaps at Bearshide (Peacehaven) and Porto Bello (Telscombe Cliffs) tracks still lead back past Telscombe village and Southease to the bridge over the Ouse below Itford Farm. These were regularly used, and later (in January 1823) the various preventive forces joined to set up an ambush at this bridge. In the event the 15 or 20 smugglers escaped along deep ditches and the goods seized hardly justified all the effort.

During the Napoleonic Wars parts of this coast came to resemble an armed camp. Barracks were built, even on the slopes above Cuckmere Haven. Following the return of peace the authorities soon discovered the value of the Coast Blockade between Sheerness and Beachy Head. A national Coast Guard was now proposed both as a

The Tiger Inn at East Dean, a convenient depot close to Birling Gap. The house called Dipperays stands just behind.

preventive force and as a valuable reserve of naval manpower. After some indecision, the Coast Blockade was extended westwards to Chichester, and the Coastguard was established further afield. Accordingly HMS *Hyperion*, under Captain Mingaye was installed in Newhaven Harbour, and by 1825 a total of 29 blockade stations were established from Beachy Head to Chichester Harbour. Their names read like a roll call of every smuggling beach in West Sussex (the list is taken from unpublished work by Mark Bullen). In the immediate area the stations were at Birling Gap, Crowlink, Cuckmere Haven, Seaford Martello, Blatchington, Newhaven, Bearshide, Porto Bello, Saltdean, Greenway (Ovingdean), Black Rock and Brighton. For good measure, guard boats patrolled offshore (one was based at Cuckmere Haven) and Riding Officers operated from East Dean, Seaford, Newhaven and Telscombe. This was formidable opposition, but the gains were still regarded as outweighing the risks of capture. Gin sold in London was being advertised as 'genuine Crowlink' and some attempts were still being made to land goods in the traditional manner. In February 1822, for example, 300 men assem-   113 bled at Crowlink but were warned off by their sentinel. The vessel tried again four nights later at Cliff Point, Seaford, and this time most of the cargo was successfully landed, but only because the patrols had been withdrawn to guard the wreck of an East Indiaman off Eastbourne.

It became standard practice to sink the tubs offshore for later collection, sometimes with humorous results. In June 1820 the master of a trading vessel from Sunderland found 62 casks which had broken adrift and were floating in the sea. He handed in 61 to the Customs at Newhaven, but maintained that one had unfortunately been stove in while getting it aboard. The uproarious behaviour of the crew belied this explanation! Another story with an ironic twist concerned a small fishing boat anchored off Seaford beach in 1820. The crew were ashore when it was searched, and vanished after it was discovered that tubs attached to a frame were moored directly under the vessel, so that they could be lifted one at a time, as local sales necessitated. A nice legal problem remained; it could not be proved that the brandy and gin had ever been on board! A further example of bare-faced opportunism concerned Thomas Vincent from Shoreham. He was quietly creeping up tubs when he was spotted by a Blockade man near Crowlink. Realising that his best chance was to put a brave face on things and claim a reward for handing in his catch to the Custom House, Vincent hoisted a tub to the masthead as a signal of his 'find'. However, it happened that another of his boats was caught soon after in Shoreham Harbour, with silks and kid gloves on board, so his claim was disallowed! Most of the goods were brought by seamen from Hastings or Bexhill and were landed by local gangs or others from Herstmonceux and Ninfield. In 1827 a Ninfield gang managed to carry away ten cartloads of goods from a landing at what is now Peacehaven.

Bribing the opposition was an alternative strategy. In September 1825 two Hailsham publicans approached a seaman from Crowlink Watch House at Cuckmere Haven and laid 20 sovereigns on the beach as an inducement to allow a quiet run. Ten months later Saunders Verrall from Exceat (the Country Park Centre) made a more generous offer to the Irishman patrolling Hope Gap. This time the reward was £40 or £50, a suit of clothes and a horse and cart so that the Blockade seamen could leave the area undetected. In both cases the smugglers were betrayed. Another trick was to divide and confuse the opposition by simultaneous landings in different places. This was tried early in 1823 when tubs were put ashore at Tide Mills at the same time as another cargo was being hauled up the cliffs just west of Newhaven. In the event both cargoes were captured and £200 in prize money was shared by the victors.

There remained the chance of running goods up the navigable rivers Ouse and Cuckmere. The course of the latter was too winding and narrow to be easily used but the Ouse was much more suitable. The trick was to let the flood tide carry a boat quickly past the men on Customs control. Sometimes this worked well and goods were landed upstream in Glynde Reach. For some years James Ashcroft and his sons collected flint pebbles from the shore and carried them upstream, their ultimate destination being the Staffordshire potteries. Eventually a tub was spotted under his cargo and Ashcroft spent the next five years in the Navy! In 1836 a particularly fine galley was rowed upstream by ten men with muffled oars, faster than the opposition could follow, but all were later captured and did six months in Lewes Gaol.

Tubs of spirit were often winched up the cliffs by derrick, and care had to be taken to remove all tell-tale signs of this. One smuggler was hit on the head by a large flint dislodged in this process near Rottingdean. At Birling Gap in 1828 a patrol surprised a smuggler who had already got 25 tubs to the top of the cliffs. He fled, and the remaining dozen fell back and shattered, with the loss of 40 gallons of overproof spirit on the pebbles! An old Folkestone smuggler spoke of 'a fraternity near Beachy Head' who disguised themselves as shepherds. While pretending to collect seabirds' eggs they excavated a platform partway down the cliff face. Then when the tide had driven the Blockade patrol from the beach below, a boat came in and the tubs were hauled up to the platform. Their scheme was eventually betrayed.

Alfriston and Rottingdean were noted as the headquarters of local gangs at this time. Stanton Collins led the men of Alfriston from Market Cross House, now the Smugglers' Inn, but detail on their activities is scanty (which could mean they were unusually clever and successful!). Edna and Mac McCarthy have been able to piece together some of Stanton's family history. His forebears came from Herstmonceux and Wartling, and his father was the butcher at Chiddingly, before buying Market Cross House. In 1822 Stanton was the tenant there and the following year he became its owner. The whole building is riddled with doorways and passages (21 rooms, 47 doors and 6 staircases, as well as cellars and a special hiding place in the roof space). This was evidently intended to baffle the opposition as well as to provide every chance of escape. Like several neighbouring buildings (which have intercommunicating attics) Market Cross House dates back centuries before Stanton Collins' time, and he must have been aware of its potential. It was his misfortune to set up in the village (as a butcher) when its prosperity was in decline, following the withdrawal of troops billeted here during the Napoleonic Wars, and 115

The Smugglers' Inn at Alfriston, formerly Market Cross House and the home of gang leader Stanton Collins.

just before the westward extension of the Coast Blockade made smuggling very hazardous.

Stanton's gang had some status in the village, and when an unseemly conflict arose at what is now the United Reformed Church, it was Stanton's men who were called to oust the interloping preacher. Apart from minor seizures in the area (12 tubs in a garden at Litlington, 6 at Jevington and one at Friston) and the burning of a local windmill when the miller was said to have refused to pass on signals, there is no evidence of Stanton's activities. His daughter was born in 1824 and a son in 1826. Then at the Winter Assize at Lewes in 1831 Stanton Collins was sentenced to seven years transportation for stealing barley from a Litlington farm. He served his sentence and returned to England to be employed as man-servant to the Rector of Herstmonceux, by 1841, and later as his footman. The last member of the Collins gang died in Eastbourne Workhouse in 1890.

The villagers of Rottingdean had also been involved in smuggling for generations. Although the coast road from Newhaven to Brighton was turnpiked in 1824, Rottingdean remained a small and isolated village until 'discovered' by the artistic and literary world some fifty years later. Sir Edward Burne-Jones came to live at North End

116

Whipping Post House, Rottingdean, the home of 'Captain' Dunk, the village butcher and local smuggler.

House, and Rudyard Kipling stayed there with his aunt in 1882, before returning to live at The Elms from 1897 to 1903. Some of the old smugglers were still alive, and their reminiscences contributed to Kipling's poem *The Smugglers' Song*. A hand-written diary of 1814 refers to 'Captain Dunk', the village butcher who lived at Whipping Post House, and had just been fined £500 and seen his ten companions consigned to Horsham gaol. Lot Elphic, who owned several fishing boats, was said to use Rottingdean windmill as one of his hiding places for contraband. 'Trunky' Thomas was one of the last of the local free traders. He was the proprietor of four bathing machines, but also kept a few cows and (more important) several fishing boats; he was a recognised local character, and appears in photographs of 1890. Smuggling at Rottingdean and Saltdean continued at least until 1850. Indeed there were 199 Coastguards operating along the stretch of coast controlled from Rottingdean in 1844, and five years later it was still felt necessary to retain the Landguard (formerly the Riding Officer). Kipling's 'Five and twenty ponies' are a fair picture of this last phase of the story here, but not of earlier mayhem and violence. 117

PLACES TO VISIT

Two circular walks

Crowlink, Birling Gap and East Dean.   National Trust carpark above Crowlink at TV 550978. Approach from the A259 turning south beside Friston Church and dew pond. (The full walk takes about two hours, but there are various options.)

Walk down the road past Crowlink Manor, and continue down to the cliff edge at Smugglers' Bottom (where there was a battery in the 1740s and a Coast Blockade Watch House in the 1820s). Walk eastwards over two of the Seven Sisters, to reach a track called Went Way beside the first house at Birling Gap. For the gap, turn right and then left to reach the hotel, carpark and steps to the beach. Went Way is the old smugglers' route up from the coast to East Dean. Follow it north as it climbs up the downs. Some 200 yards beyond a red barn the ways divide. The path straight ahead leads back to the Crowlink carpark; Went Way forks to the right and descends quickly to East Dean village, and the Tiger Inn. The house Dipperays can be seen behind the inn. A footpath leads up to Friston Church, where the more northerly of two box tombs east of the church is the grave of Exciseman Fletcher. Turn left here for the carpark; the contraband was carried north to Jevington, or along Old Willingdon Road over the Downs.

Cuckmere Haven and Seaford Head
Carpark on Seaford Head at TV 505980. Approach from Seaford along Chyngton Road, turning right up the hill to a prominent barn. (The full route takes about 75 minutes.) Walk down to the Coast-guard cottages on the fringe of Cuckmere Haven (the Coast Blockade Watch House is the lowest building); the view includes all the Seven Sisters. Follow the cliff path round Seaford Head Nature Reserve, passing Hope Gap and continuing to the summit overlooking Sea-ford, Newhaven and the coast further west. Retrace your steps to the eastern edge of the golf course, turning left and later right (along the runway of a 1940s airfield) to the carpark.

Other Visits and View Points

Alfriston
Carpark in village. Well worth exploring for its many old buildings, apart from its smuggling history. Notice particularly the Market Cross Inn, where Stanton Collins lived from 1822 to 1831. The Star is a 15th century inn thought to have been used by pilgrims. The figurehead outside is from a Dutch ship wrecked at Cuckmere Haven

In the 17th century. The George also dates from the 15th century, and was later a coaching inn. Several other old buildings have intercommunicating attics, and both the Tudor Cafe and the Moonrakers are traditionally associated with smuggling. (In the moonrakers story, usually told in collection with Wiltshire but also claimed by Piddinghoe near Newhaven, men retrieving tubs from a pond acted the role of village idiots when surprised by an Exciseman, and claimed to be catching a cheese – the moon's reflection.) The Priest's House (National Trust) beside the church is well worth a visit.

Bo Peep Picnic Site

On the South Downs crest at TQ 495050. Approach from the A27, turning south between Selmeston and Alciston. An excellent viewpoint on one of the smugglers' regular routes inland (and also on the South Downs Way).

Rottingdean

Carparking adjoining the A259. To explore the old village, walk up the High Street and round the Green. Notice particularly Tallboys, built in 1780 as the old Custom House, and the Black Horse Inn (once partly a forge) which was a smugglers' rendezvous. Whipping Post House, the home of 'Captain' Dunk, formerly stood beside the stocks and whipping post. North End House, Hillside and Challoners (the manor house) stand round the Green. St Margaret's church has windows made by William Morris, to designs by Sir Edward Burne-Jones. Kipling lived at The Elms from 1897 to 1902. The Grange is now the public library, but was Thomas Hooker's rectory, complete with cellars!

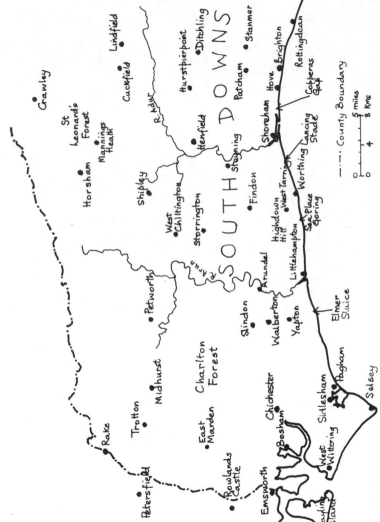

Places associated with smuggling in West Sussex.

8

The West Sussex Coast from Brighton to Pagham Harbour

The story of smuggling along the West Sussex coast has been relatively neglected, and there are fewer reports of what took place largely because the preventive net was less tightly drawn here, at least until the 1820s. Nevertheless the opportunities were very great. Shoreham is the nearest Channel port to London, and the great uninterrupted sweep of sand and shingle beaches stretching for almost thirty miles offered excellent landing prospects. This was an empty coast before 1700 and under the threat of attack not only from France, but by the sea itself. The terrible storm of 1703 (which sank so many vessels on the Goodwin Sands) tore away the beach from below the cliffs at Brighton, where the fishing boats had previously been drawn up. At Heene (Worthing) the coast was cut back by some 55 yards in less than a century, and early roads along the coast were regularly destroyed. As a result, the small villages lay a short distance inland, and it was from communities such as West Blatchinton (Brighton) or Lancing, Sompting and West Tarring (Worthing) that men came down to the shore by night to run tea and brandy. Brighton (or Brighthelmston) was reduced from an important fishing port of some 4000 souls in 1650 to a mere 2000 poverty-stricken inhabitants a century later, when a visitor described them as very needy and wretched, but skilled in nautical pursuits and in cheating the Customs men.

The port of Shoreham was also menaced by the sea as shingle was driven eastwards across the Adur estuary, causing silting of the harbour and shifting of its mouth. Old Shoreham had been superseded by New Shoreham (newly-built in 1096!) and this in turn was partly destroyed by the sea in 1348. Problems continued, and during most of the smuggling years the river Adur entered the sea at what is now the western edge of Hove. The Adur was navigable, and contraband could be carried some ten miles inland to the ancient river port of Steyning and the wharves at Bineham Bridge serving Henfield. The river Arun was also navigable, and after 1816 its waters were linked to the Thames by a canal to the river Wey. At its mouth was Littlehampton, the small outport for the town of Arundel.

Since the West Wessex coast is free of rocky headlands and cliffs, the gently shelving shores were ideal for beaching a vessel or offloading its cargo into small boats. In the days before the groynes and promenades were built at Worthing, for example, an early guidebook described the shore as smooth as a carpet and level as a lawn! It seems likely that virtually the entire coast between Brighton and Selsey Bill was used to run goods at one time or another, but certain favourite landing sites were particularly important. These were probably chosen because of easy access to a series of ancient droveways running over the South Downs and into the Weald. Confirmation that these were the smuggling 'black spots' comes from the choice of sites for the establishment of Watch Houses when the Coast Blockade was extended along this coast in the 1820s.

Goods were certainly landed on the beach at Brighton, and sometimes taken directly into inns and shops within the Lanes, but a much better landing place was at the foot of Hove Street in Hove, a site now submerged under blocks of flats and a dual-carriageway section of King's Esplanade. Up to the time when this spot became a base for the preventivemen, Hove was no more than a straggle of houses along Hove Street, with convenient hiding places at the Ship Inn and Red Lion. St Andrew's Church (before its restoration in 1836) was also used; a well-known story is told of the vicar who held services on alternate Sundays here and at neighbouring Preston Church. On one occasion he mistakenly insisted on trying to preach at Hove when it was Preston's turn, only to find the nave stacked with tubs and the pulpit full of tea! At the junction of Old Shoreham Road and Sackville Road there was a cleverly disguised entrance to a double cave, cut into the back of a chalk pit. The route over the Downs went on through Goldstone Bottom and past West Blatchington, where the church was again used for storage, and so past Devil's Dyke heading for Hurstpierpoint and Cuckfield.

Just inside what was then the Adur river mouth was Copperas Gap, now transformed under the buildings of Portslade. This was another favourite landing place, from which downland tracks led inland towards Henfield and Cowfold. The first turnpike road linking Brighton and London later went this way, past Erringham Farm and over Beeding Hill to Bramber. Accordingly the ghost of a headless lady at Erringham and a phantom Dutchman at Copperas Gap were invented to discourage casual investigation!

An even better smuggling beach west of the river Adur was then known as Lancing Shops. It had once been Lancing Stade, and was evidently an old-established landing site; today Lancing Sailing Club premises stand on this spot, and one can still appreciate its value. Immediately behind the beach is a rough but embanked track which continues (as Old Salts Road today) on slightly higher land along the edge of the marshes, leading directly towards the Sussex Pad Inn. The present building on this site replaced the notorious old inn, which was burned down in 1905, but the out-buildings where contraband was stored are still there. The inn took its name from the causeway built on faggots across the marsh, which led to the ferry across to Old Shoreham. Until Old Shoreham Bridge was built in 1782, there was no other crossing point below Beeding Bridge, so the Sussex Pad Inn stood in a crucial position on the road network. A very ancient track climbs up the South Downs from behind the inn. This was used by smugglers, who appear to have had depots at Findon and Steyning, and there are records of fights and seizures at Wiston and Chanctonbury further north. For some years there was a gang based at Shipley which met at Spear Hill to plan landings at Shoreham or Lancing, and there are known to have been depots at Ashington, Shipley and Broadbridge Farm.

The beach at Worthing was a good landing place, and Sea Place at Goring, further west, was at the heart of regular smuggling runs. The shore is still open here, but the site of Sea Place is submerged under modern housing. Sea Place itself was a group of ancient farm buildings on a moated site, which must have provided excellent storage; its existence is perpetuated today in three street names: Sea Place, Smugglers' Walk and Moat Walk. Courtlands, the other large house nearby, is also said to have had a secret tunnel. The Worthing and Goring beaches were regularly used by villagers from Durrington, Salvington, Broadwater, Sompting and (above all) West Tarring, who were enthusiastic participants in the trade. From Worthing the obvious route north was through Findon and Washington. That from Goring and Ferring led past the natural lookout point and signal station provided by Highdown Hill. This isolated summit was to figure in various episodes, and an eccentric miller called John Oliver lived here for many years before his death in 1793. His sympathies may be deduced from a device on his house which showed a Customs officer with upraised sword pursuing a smuggler, and an old woman at his heels beating the officer with her broom! He kept his coffin under his bed, and had his table tomb constructed well in advance (it must have provided at least limited storage!). Miller Oliver was a well known local character, and we can assume that he acted as signaller for the smugglers; it was common practice to use the set of windmill   123

Old Shoreham Bridge over the river Adur. This toll bridge, opened in 1782, leads to the Sussex Pad Inn.

sails according to a pre-arranged code. From the north side of High-down Hill a bridleway still marks the line of an early road over Blackpatch Hill past Sullington, the edge of Storrington and on to West Chiltington, a village which became a smugglers' headquarters in the 1720s. There was ingenious storage behind a mill wheel at Coolham, on the route to Horsham, an important market town closely involved in the trade.

Almost the only stretch of shore line in West Sussex which still remains undeveloped and conveys something of the character and atmosphere of this coast as the smugglers knew it lies between Littlehampton and Middleton. At what is now Climping beach, a straggling line of trees backs the shore, and the impression is heightened by old farm buildings and the apparently ancient Bailiffscourt. In fact this is a reconstruction on a historic site, using ancient materials. It was created between 1929 and 1934 for Lord and Lady Moyne, and even the trees were moved from further inland! The smugglers particularly favoured Elmer Sluice, just west of here and on the eastern edge of Middleton. Between four and five tons of tea were brought ashore at Elmer Sluice from the cutter *Samuel Betts* of Rye in

1745. A large landing party was obviously required for this, and labourers came from every village in the district (including the rat catcher from Aldingbourne!) and from as far away as Chichester and Sidlesham to the west, and Stopham and Arundel to the east. This particular landing went very badly wrong, and 36 smugglers were captured, most of whom had carried firearms and therefore faced the death penalty.

Of course smuggling in West Sussex was well established long before 1745. The illegal exporting of wool from Shoreham began as early as 1274 and had continued for centuries. It was still being carried on around 1740 when (according to the evidence of a former smuggler preserved in the Goodwood papers) twelve packs of wool were collected at Fittleworth near Petworth, and taken by waggon '... to a wood near Hidower Mill in Sussex, where it lay for a week.' It was then carried to a vessel among fishing boats off Worthing and 'Jack-Come-Last of Burdhole in Clacton' (Birdshole in Clayton, north of Brighton) took it to France and sold it for £13 a pack. As on the coast further east, French vessels came touting for custom, and offering silks and brandy in return for the wool. In 1704 £4000 worth of French silk was seized near Steyning, and in 1719 it was reported that French vessels lay at anchor for days close to the shore, so that their customers could row out to make purchases.

As far as the prevention of smuggling was concerned at this time, Henry Baker, the Supervisor of Riding Officers, said of the sole Custom House officer at Littlehampton that he was '... no more use for this service than a gull on the beach'. (John Collier was later to be offered the doubtful services of a former smuggler-turned-Riding-Officer for duties here.) However, several individuals were to emerge as dedicated 'smuggler hunters'. John Jarrett, Lieutenant Jekyll of Brigadier Groves' Regiment, and John Rogers, a hop grower working in the Revenue service were to play a significant role as violence increased after 1720. Their difficulty lay in the attitude of local magistrates, who had every reason to fear retaliation by the smuggling community if they dared to imprison one of its members. No doubt many magistrates were also regular customers. Moreover, though John Jarrett had the necessary legal powers of arrest, John Rogers' authority was less certainly based. Despite this state of affairs, smugglers were committed to Horsham gaol. Some were hanged on Horsham Common, and it is on record that condemned men shuffled up the nave of Horsham church in their fetters.

The escalation of violence in West Sussex was the inevitable consequence of the involvement of major gangs from outside the region. The first recorded instance of this concerned a gang from inland Hampshire known as the Farnham Blacks, who tried their hands at 125 smuggling in West Sussex before 1720, apparently as an alternative to their more usual occupations of poaching and deer stealing. Soon after this, members of the Mayfield gang were working on the West Sussex coast from bases in West Chiltington and Horsham. This gang's story is complicated by confusion over names and aliases, and by the repetition of arrests, escapes and re-arrests. In essence the gang had risen to power in the owling trade but progressed to landing tea and spirits on the Romney Marsh and East Sussex coasts. Their acknowledged leader was Gabriel Tomkins, and other important members included his half brother Edward, Jacob Walter, Thomas Bigg and Francis Hammond. By 1721 most of these men had been arrested but regained their freedom one way or another, and Edward Tomkins had a price on his head for tying up a Customs man while brandy was being run on Seaford beach. John Jarrett had already arrested Francis Hammond twice (only to see him rescued in Mayfield on the second occasion when Gabriel and his brother came with blacked faces and suitably armed). Now John Rogers, assisted by Lieutenant Jekyll, but without the necessary warrants, decided to round up the villains and claim the reward.

The first opportunity came in August 1721 when Edward Tomkins walked past John Rogers' house. Rogers and several companions, including the local constable, followed Edward Tomkins to a house in West Chiltington, where he spent the night. Early next morning John Rogers called on his victim to surrender, and when the smuggler emerged half dressed, he was wounded and captured in a nearby field. Eager to claim his reward, John Rogers took Tomkins before the Horsham magistrate Mr Lindfield, but was promptly put in prison for making an unlawful arrest. The magistrate did place Edward Tomkins in the care of the local constable, however, but Tomkins immediately escaped. Smuggler-hunter Rogers was thereupon freed. Eight days later John Rogers made another attempt, this time with the help of Lieutenant Jekyll and a party of Grenadiers. They surrounded an inn at West Chiltington and captured five smugglers and thirty-four horses, complete with pack saddles. This time the Horsham magistrates gaoled one smuggler but freed the rest 'for want of sufficient evidence'. The five smugglers captured on this occasion had been on their way to meet a cargo at Goring. Fifteen other gang members had already reached the coast the previous night, and, finding a Customs officer on watch, had bound him and thrown him into a ditch. The expected vessel duly arrived, but because the smugglers' horses had been seized by Rogers at West Chiltington, a successful landing was impossible, and the ship sailed for an alternative landing site.

126   A month later John Rogers tried yet again, and with success. With

Jekyll and the Grenadiers he came upon Edward's brother Gabriel Tomkins and other smugglers at Burwash in East Sussex, followed them, and finally surrounded them in a lane at Nutley on Ashdown Forest. The Horsham magistrates felt compelled to uphold the law on this occasion, but Gabriel Tomkins, who was said to be worth £10,000, had little difficulty in bribing his gaoler. He was recaptured, and at last tried in London; his sentence was seven years transportation, but by giving invaluable information to his captors he was presently at liberty yet again. Meanwhile John Rogers and Lieutenant Jekyll went back to the task of rounding up the other suspects. In one four-day expedition they succeeded in capturing two smugglers at Pagham, two at Rustington, two at Kingston, one at Preston and two near Arundel. All went before magistrates at the White Horse Inn at Horsham; it is no surprise that the case against them was promptly dismissed because the smugglers were not caught in the act, and John Rogers was whipped for his presumption. But at least the Mayfield gang had been effectively broken up by the capture of Gabriel Tomkins in September 1721. Though he and his henchman Jacob Walter were working again by 1724, it was in East Sussex and they were both captured there in 1729. (It was following this arrest that Gabriel Tomkins again talked his way out of gaol and went on to become a Customs officer at Dartford and eventually a highwayman!)

Violence and bloodshed in West Sussex became serious once more after 1740, and the records made it certain that on occasion men from Groombridge, Hawkhurst and Hastings were involved. A typically vicious episode took place near Arundel in 1741, when the local Supervisor of Riding Officers, his assistants and nine soldiers went to intercept an expected landing. In the battle which developed the smugglers beat to death two of the officers, before escaping with their goods. There is no record that those involved in this crime were ever brought to justice. In April 1744 Dragoon Michael Bath was mortally wounded during a landing at Sea Place, Goring. According to the sworn testimony of a witness, John Collier's relative Thomas Holman of Hastings took part. (He was later sentenced to transportation for this, having been reprieved from death through John Collier's intervention.) John Mills from Trotton in West Sussex was also involved. He was later to be executed for a particularly savage murder at Slindon near Chichester, during the trials which finally broke the Hawkhurst gang. Thomas Ward, otherwise Bulverhythe Tom from Groombridge, was also suspected of involvement in the Sea Place killing.

In another encounter near Shoreham, three officers who tried unsuccessfully to seize goods being landed there were overpowered, beaten and taken back to Hawkhurst. Later they were compelled to 127

Southdown House, Patcham, Brighton. Built in 1711, with large cellars, escape tunnels and metal latticework reinforcing the doors and shutters.

help with a landing of tea near Dungeness. Apparently the intention had been to carry them over to France, which was then at war with Britain.

If outsiders were responsible for the worst violence, there is plenty of evidence that local men were actively involved. The thirty-six smugglers captured at Elmer Sluice in 1745 were all from West Sussex. About the same time a gang from the Steyning area was running goods at Lancing. Hugh Green from Applesham near Lancing was said to have been responsible for the death of a dragoon on the beach there. Moreover, the escalation of violence coincided with clear indications that Jacobite sympathisers were active in West Sussex. Thus James Bishop of Parham with his servant and James Ibbotson from near Arundel, tried to persuade the smugglers of Hooe near Pevensey to take them to France to join Bonnie Prince Charlie, before the rebellion of 1745, but were betrayed.

In a bid to stem the collapse of law and order, Major Battine, Surveyor General of Riding Officers in Sussex, was forced to appeal for additional military help, and in 1745 the government responded by sending two regiments of dragoons and one of foot soldiers to the major smuggling counties of Sussex, Kent and Essex. In West Sussex these men were based at Arundel, Petworth, Midhurst, Petersfield and Chichester. At this point the Duke of Richmond, then living at Goodwood House, began what amounted to a personal campaign against the leading smugglers. Despite attempts to blackmail him, he devoted the last three years of his life to hunting down the worst villains.

An uneasy peace descended on the West Sussex coast following the great trials of 1749, which broke up the major gangs and their West Sussex collaborators. No blood was shed on the beaches for six years; thereafter the free trade began again and was soon to become just as widespread, if less wantonly cruel. By the 1770s contraband was coming ashore in huge quantities, and violence and lawlessness reached a peak around 1780. However, in Brighton fortunes revived as the town developed into a fashionable resort. Dr Russell published his treatise on the values of seawater (in Latin!) in 1750, and the number of visitors grew rapidly thereafter. The success of the resort was assured after the visit of the Prince of Wales in 1783. These developments affected the smuggling community in several ways. Packet boats sailing across the Channel provided their passengers with excellent opportunities to acquire continental fashions, and in 1776 lace worth £1000 was found in a chaise on a vessel returning from Dieppe. The presence of the court at Brighton created a lively market for luxuries which could be met by clandestine landings at Shoreham, Hove or Rottingdean. Brighton itself was becoming too well organised for the easy landing of goods on the town beach, although minor incidents still occurred, and were reported in the local press.

In the villages behind Brighton things continued much as before. On the Stanmer estate (now the University of Sussex) it was said that everyone took part except its owner, Henry Pelham. The estate bailiff was one of the organisers, the chaplain was injured on his way back from a run at Rottingdean, and there were depots in the woods above Stanmer House. The smuggling community at Patcham further west was on the regular route over to Ditchling. Daniel Skayles' tombstone in Patcham churchyard records that he was 'unfortunately shot' in 1796 as a result of one such clandestine venture.

It is a remarkable tribute to men in the Revenue service that they were prepared to tackle large convoys of well armed men, and to resist the intimidation to which they were constantly subjected. In 1774 the Riding Officer at Salvington near Worthing was found hanging in an outhouse, and in 1778 two officers were lured out of Horsham and then set upon by sixty smugglers and left for dead. Reports speak of battles at Wiston Park near Steyning, Staplefield Common and Hor-

The beach known to the smugglers as Lancing Shops, from which contraband went to the Sussex Pad Inn.

sham Common during these years. In December 1778, when a gang of nearly two hundred men rode openly through the centre of Henfield, they took with them in addition to their goods, seven captured Revenue officers whom they later freed unharmed. (The more discreet smugglers' route through the Henfield area lay across the common further east.) The full measure of prevailing lawlessness in these years is reflected in a report sent to Lord Shelburne as Prime Minister. In December 1782 three large smuggling vessels were seen lying off the coast, and several hundred horses waited on the beach near Shoreham. The Excise Supervisor at Lewes was told that there was enough tea, coffee, spirits, wines, muslins and other goods to make 3000 horse-loads, and he was called on to attack the 500 smugglers taking part in the operation. Prudently he declined to do so 'for want of a sufficient military force to support him'.

In response to this situation the chief Revenue officer at Horsham, a Mr Walter, evolved a plan to counter the smugglers. He recruited paid spies, and with his assistants Mr Hubbard and Mr Jenden and some twenty dragoons, he developed a trained and uniformed band of men, capable of acting on the information he received. He was particularly successful in capturing goods being taken for concealment in Ashdown and St Leonard's Forests. In the summer of 1781, for example, he made a succession of seizures at Crawley, Worth, Reigate and Ditchling. The records of seizures continued over the next three years at a series of towns from Guildford and Mayfield to Bolney, Petworth and Petersfield. On occasion Walter's men captured as much as 2½ tons of tea in a single month. It is difficult to avoid the conclusion that Mr Walter was perhaps more interested in making a handsome living from the rewards for his captures, than in the defeat of the smugglers. His men did not escape unscathed. In July 1783 Mr Hubbard and five others were wounded in a battle at Eartham near Chichester. Ten months later Mr Hubbard was again involved in a fight at Lancing. His horse was captured, and he had to wade across the river Adur in water up to his neck in order to escape. Ordinary citizens were becoming disenchanted with these activities, and actions for trespass were brought by a tradesman at Hurstpierpoint and a farmer at Portslade. Then in June 1787 Philip Jenden killed a smuggler while leading the attack against a gang running goods at Hove. He was arrested for murder, and although he was eventually pardoned and released, it was not before he had been sentenced to be hanged and his body used for medical research! The Member of Parliament for Horsham took an unfavourable view of Mr Walter's private army, and the troop was disbanded about 1790.

These years saw other threats to the free traders. More soldiers were now stationed along these shores because of attacks by French privateers, and those at Brighton were willing to help with the capture of tubs, so long as they could sample the goods on the way to Shoreham Custom House! Naval vessels also intercepted the smuggling craft, but there is the less creditable record that eighteen sailors in naval uniform, mounted and armed, successfully carried their own load of contraband through Buxted and into Ashdown Forest! Four Revenue vessels regularly patrolled off the coast, but it was still possible in 1803 for fashionable visitors walking on Brighton Steyne to see tubs being openly brought ashore by fishermen, and shared with Revenue officers!

Smuggling increased once more as soldiers and sailors returned home after victory at Waterloo. After 1818 free traders from Kent and East Sussex, who were now harrassed on their own shores by the patrols of the Coast Blockade, could hope for greater freedom from interference in West Sussex. However, the extension of the Blockade to Chichester by 1824 closed that loophole. There were still opportunities to bribe men in the preventive service, and it was reported that the guards at Brighton had come to an arrangement with the smugglers to capture a proportion of the tubs, and let the rest through. Accordingly official exhortations to show more zeal in the service were sent out. Despite this, in 1827 some 200 tubs of spirit were brazenly landed opposite the fine new houses of Brunswick Terrace at Hove, and other cargoes still found their way into the cellars of the Ship Inn at Brighton. Two drapers of North Street in Brighton were particularly anxious to supply the clothes which fashionable society demanded. Mr Weston at 18 and 19 North Street had a kitchen range on wheels which could be moved to reveal his stock of silk and lace. He was fined £10,000 and paid up without difficulty. The activities of his neighbour, Mr Powell at number 16, were revealed by an invoice and goods discovered on a vessel at Newhaven in 1822. This single consignment included a wide range of articles from opera glasses to musical boxes and bracelets of human hair, but the most valuable items were 950 yards of silk, 292 yards of silk lawn, and over 200 pairs of leather gloves.

As elsewhere, the method now used was to sow a crop (sink tubs of spirit at sea) for later retrieval. The discovery of a rich new source of oysters in 1823 provided exactly the right cover for these operations. Worthing was now developing rapidly as a resort; the Steyne here dates from 1813, and the Esplanade was completed in 1821. There were a number of incidents here in the 1820s, but the major battle took place just after the Coastguards had taken over from the Blockade. Some 300 tubs of spirit were run ashore at 3 a.m. in bright moonlight in February 1832 at the centre of Worthing's seafront, and carried through the Steyne. Following standard practice, the landing party was flanked by men wielding bats and staves, but the Coastguards saw the convoy and fired to summon assistance. Lieutenant Henderson and four other officers joined them, and a running battle developed along Worthing High Street and the surrounding side streets, as the smugglers used their local knowledge to escape down passageways. The gang reached open country (where today the High Street bends round into North Street) and continued along a field track (now Upper High Street), but were delayed by a footbridge over the Teville Brook. William Cowerson, a stonemason from Steyning whose legitimate trade was repairing West Tarring church, took charge of the rearguard action. He broke Lieutenant Henderson's arm with his bat, but Henderson had his gun in the other hand, and shot and killed Cowerson. The smuggler stonemason lies buried in Steyning churchyard. This was effectively the last smuggling battle in West Sussex, but it was not the end of the trade. There was another important run through the grounds of Beach House in Worthing in November 1838, when the Coastguards captured half the spirits but the men escaped.

All standard ways of running contraband ashore had now become too difficult, but there was no cause for complacency within the preventive service. In 1849 it was still felt necessary to continue the

Boatyards at Littlehampton on the river Arun today; the beach and riverside were notorious smuggling haunts.

Landguard (formerly the Riding Officer) at Littlehampton, and to base a total of 176 Coastguards there. Two stories from the 1850s show the ingenuity still being practised. In August 1855 a circus came to Shoreham, and complementary tickets were given to all civic dignitaries and, of course, the Coastguards. At an appropriate moment a vessel ostensibly laden with stone (but apparently carrying 14 tons of tobacco) tied up beside the Custom House Quay. Bales of tobacco were quietly transferred into barges and carried up to Beeding chalk pits on the flood tide, and then loaded into four horse-drawn vans. One of these is known to have gone via Horsham and was later confiscated at Guildford. Another went via Hurstpierpoint and Cuckfield, but nothing else was ever found.

William Albery, the local historian at Horsham, investigated the saga of the Allens' malthouses there. (When Albery wrote in the 1930s it was still possible to identify a number of Horsham buildings known to have been used to conceal goods; recent development has destroyed this evidence.) Alfred Allen of Horsham and Dennett Allen of West Chiltington built up a remarkable organisation over ten years, and made huge profits by mixing locally-made malt with equal quantities of its smuggled equivalent. By 1857 they owned five malthouses and three farms. At this point their activities leaked out because they were

133

blackmailed by one of their employees (who wanted the money to build a station hotel at Worthing!) Prolonged investigation finally revealed that a concealed vault had been constructed at each malt-house. £12,000 worth of malt was seized and taken by special train to London! Meanwhile the Allens fled to France, and then threw off pursuit by returning immediately to London, and sailing from Liverpool to America. They were found guilty (in their absence) and fined £370,000. Since there was no extradition procedure for this offence, the fine was eventually reduced to a mere £10,000, which the Allens promptly paid, and returned to England!

The last major seizure of contraband spirits in West Sussex took place at Arundel in 1860, but there is little doubt that smaller scale smuggling, particularly of tobacco, continued.

PLACES TO VISIT

Two longer walks along routes used by the smugglers which can be tackled from several points:

Patcham to Ditchling Beacon
Limited roadside parking near Patcham Church. (TQ 303092) or N.T. carpark on Ditchling Beacon (TQ 333130). Starting from the south, first explore Patcham. Southdown House in Old London Road, built in 1711 and still a private house, has large cellars, a grille of metal bars inset into doors and shutters, and a tunnel which formerly led to the Black Lion Inn (now a paint works). Patcham Place, now the Youth Hostel, also had escape tunnels. The building is much older than its eighteenth century facade suggests. Anthony Stapley, one of the signatories of Charles I's death warrant, lived here. Daniel Skayles' gravestone is just behind the north wall of the church. The public bridleway to Ditchling sets off from Vale Road, just above the church. This became a turnpike under an Act of 1770. The route passes close to the Chattri, a monument to Hindu and Sikh soldiers of the First World War who died in Brighton Hospital. At Keymer Post, on the downland crest, the smugglers descended directly north-eastwards to Ditchling, but it is easier today to turn east along the South Downs Way past the local nature reserve, to the viewpoint indicator on Ditchling Beacon. Ditchling itself is full of ancient buildings and is well worth visiting. There are no obvious signs from times when armed convoys rode through, or when it was said that every man in the church choir was a smuggler. The gibbet stood on Ditchling Common.

Lancing – Steyning Bowl – Chanctonbury
Limited roadside parking by the Pad Inn (TQ 200061) and carparks at Steyning Bowl (TQ 163005) and Chanctonbury (TQ 146126). The start at Lancing is by public bridleway which turns left from just inside the gateway of Lancing College. The track aims for the skyline and curves slowly to the right to join the South Downs Way. The northern approach is from A283 (sign to Chanctonbury), following the obvious track through woods to the crest of the downs.

Picnic Sites and View Points

Mill Hill, Shoreham. Carpark on road to Beeding Hill at TQ 213074. Approach from Upper Shoreham Road (NOT A27) following picnic and Truleigh Hill signs. Excellent views across the Adur valley to sites used by the smugglers. Goods were hidden at Old Erringham below. New Erringham Farm was a coaching inn on the first turnpike from London and Horsham to Shoreham and Brighton.
Highdown Hill and the Miller's Tomb. Carpark at TQ 608042. Approach from dual-carriageway section of the A2032, turning north at sign to Highdown Gardens. For the Miller's Tomb, follow the track north-westwards towards the summit. There is much else to see. The gardens, maintained by Worthing Council, are excellent and contain a cafe. Highdown Hill is also an important archaeological site, crowned by an Iron Age rampart, but also including remains from Bronze Age, Roman and Saxon periods.
Chantry Post above Storrington. Carpark at TQ 087120. Approach from the A283, turning south (sign to Chantry Hill) on eastern edge of Storrington. The smugglers crossed the South Downs here from Highdown Hill (just visible to the south) on their way to West Chiltington and Horsham, due north of here.

Other Interesting Visits:

West Chiltington (best linked to visiting Chantry Post). Parking near church at TQ 090185. A delightful village, with over fifty timber-framed houses and interesting thirteenth century frescoes in the church. There are no obvious reminders of the many smuggling episodes which took place here.
Climping Beach. Carpark (charge) at TQ 006007, Atherington. Approach from the A259 turning south at sign, two miles west of Littlehampton. The only undeveloped stretch of coast, and certainly one the smugglers used. Elmer Sluice lies about a mile to the west.
Marlipins Museum, Shoreham. Public carparks in Shoreham. Open

daily, main season only. This fascinating medieval building was probably once the Custom House. The collection includes items from Shoreham's seafaring past, some excellent old maps, and an oil painting of the wreck of the *Nympha Americana* in 1747, showing wreckers at work below Crowlink.

9

The Chichester Area and the Breakup of the Worst Smuggling Gangs

One story above all others dominates the record of smuggling along the Sussex/Hampshire border, for it was here in January 1749 that the villainies of the Hawkhurst Gang and their locally-based associates were revealed at the great Special Assize in Chichester. Parts of that story are well known from two contemporary records. A recent and detailed account appears in *Honest Thieves. The Violent Heyday of English Smuggling*, by F F Nichols. I have summarised here the more bestial episodes, and linked together the various trials of the period (in London, Rochester, Lewes and East Grinstead as well as Chichester) which finally broke the smuggling mafia of these years.

Needless to say, contraband was coming ashore in the Chichester area long before 1749, and continued to do so for the next century. To understand why, one has only to look at the character of the coastline from Portsmouth round Selsey Bill to Pagham Harbour. Though these shores were further from the main continental suppliers and the London market, they had considerable natural advantages. The great tidal estuaries which form Langstone, Chichester and Pagham Harbours provided sheltered and secluded landing sites, and the tide race through each narrow entrance could be used to carry in rafts of floating tubs, after the method commonly adopted in Dorset to ferry goods into Poole and Christchurch Harbours. In addition there were excellent open shores, partially sheltered by the Isle of Wight, on which to beach a vessel, especially near Selsey and on Hayling Island. The proximity of the Isle of Wight was particularly useful after 1840 when the mainland coast was generally too well guarded. Smuggling on Wight continued into the 1860s, and it was relatively easy to bring goods across in small boats from the harbour at St Helens.

The great length of shoreline, with its muddy creeks and tidal estuaries, made the enforcement of law and order particularly dif- 137

The Smugglers' Stone on the Broyle at Chichester. This modern notice reproduces the inscription on the stone, erected in 1749, which is now difficult to read.

ficult. Think of the problems faced by the lone Riding Officer based at Emsworth around 1750! The coast road we now call the A27 was at times impassable because of flooding at the river mouths, and the recognised alternative pack horse route from Havant to Chichester ran inland via Rowland's Castle, Stansted and Funtington. There was no land link to Hayling Island or Selsey. A causeway ran to Selsey from Sidlesham, and there were others from Emsworth and Langstone to Hayling Island, but there was no bridge to the island before 1850. Small wonder therefore that Selsey Bill and Hayling Island were notorious landing sites, and Emsworth, Rowland's Castle, Langstone and Farlington further west were major centres.

The land behind these coasts is fertile farmland, and in the eighteenth century this was still mostly in open fields interspered by large areas of common. Much common land remained unenclosed until the early nineteenth century (the 670 acres at Selsey were enclosed under an Act of 1819). The commons provided excellent opportunities for concealment, and it is known that huge storage depots were excavated in the soft subsoil of the southern part of Hayling Island. The South Downs along the Hampshire border are much more extensively wooded than further east. Charlton Forest, north of Chichester, and the Forest of Bere further west had been important hunting grounds for many centuries, and a number of estates had been developed here by 1700, belonging to noble lords devoted to the chase. It was these men, in their capacity as JPs and magistrates, who played a significant role in the smuggling story. In particular, the Second Duke of Richmond carried out what amounted to a personal campaign against the leaders of the main gangs, from 1723 when he inherited Goodwood House, until his death in 1750. The Dukes of Norfolk at Arundel Castle took a more ambivalent line, often insisting on their ancient manorial right to claim goods washed ashore. In 1753 an embarrassed Collector of Customs wrote to his superiors about 143 hogsheads of French wine from a wrecked Dutch ship which the Duke had locked in a barn on Hayling Island, and refused to hand over.

Against this background, the smuggling which was well established before 1700, here as elsewhere, was the illegal exporting of wool. Chichester was for centuries one of the staple ports from which it was lawful to ship out wool. The trade was handled through the small outports at Dell Quay, Bosham and later, Emsworth. Alongside this legal trade there is evidence of its extensive smuggled counterpart, particularly from the Selsey area. At the height of the trade around 1720 (according to Neville Williams) one skipper took a vessel to France and back every week for five years, and each night a convoy of waggons passed between the Sussex coast and Selsey Bill. A local farmer was said to have made £10,000 profit in six years of part-time operations, and Henry Chitty, an owler previously operating on Romney Marsh, transferred his activities to Selsey, no doubt for greater freedom from interference. The Board of Customs in London sent repeated instructions to its officials at Southampton and Portsmouth urging their greatest vigilance to prevent the trade. In 1759, during the Seven Years War, they added a warning that packages, said to contain hardware from Birmingham and Sheffield, in fact held concealed guns and swords being shipped to France. In 1771 they were still commenting on the great quantities of wool being carried illegally to Boulogne from Sussex.

The large scale importing of contraband along all the shores bordering the Solent was well established by the early eighteenth century. In 1719 the Board of Customs told the Collector at the port of Southampton '... about a fortnight since there was on your coast a vessell, pretending to be Dutch, but with an English Master, out of which there was sold in a few days at least £6000 worth of calicoes, silks and spices ... which goods were run ashore and conveyed into the country by a hundred and sometimes 500 horse in a night, and being informed that the same ship will shortly come again on your coast ... we direct you to excite the several officers under your care to do their utmost to prevent the same.' Despite such warnings the traffic and the violence associated with it increased. In 1743, for example, a large gang of smugglers from Aldingbourne brought 2000 pounds of tea ashore near West Wittering. It was said that due to the laxity of the Riding Officers at Portsea and Cosham, one could buy lace, muslins, gin, brandy, tobacco and tea more cheaply here than in France.

The Duke of Richmond at Goodwood House had his own problems. In November 1735 he received a letter demanding 250 guineas (which would later be returned with 50 guineas interest!) '... for hear are 2 hundred and 50 of us, and in too days time we can raise our company to 6 hundred so if you do not deliver your money quitly we will destroy all you have and we will shoot his Grace whearever we sees him....' In view of the Duke's implacable opposition to smuggling, it is unlikely that the request was satisfied! However, eight years later his own servants were found to have concealed tea on the premises and were selling it from Goodwood House itself. By that time the notorious Hawkhurst men were infiltrating the local gangs and even extending their operations as far west as Dorset. In 1748 they were held responsible for the death of a Riding Officer, shot on Selhurst Common close to Goodwood. The previous year several of the Duke's servants (a huntsman and whippers-in of hounds) were suspected of involvement with the gangs, and the Duke had to write in their defence to explain their presence at Lyndhurst in the New

Forest. He said they were looking after his hunting interests there, and whipper-in Thomas Perrin 'took a horse to be shod'. In view of the role of another Chichester man also called Perrin in the tale which follows, one wonders whether the Duke was being entirely honest.

The story of events leading up to the great Chichester trial of 1749 properly starts in Dorset, but involved both a local gang from the Hampshire border and the Hawkhurst men from Kent, then led by Thomas Kingsmill and William Fairall. According to testimony later given by John Diamond, who took part, the two groups came to an agreement with William Hollace of Rye (who owned a small vessel) to go to Guernsey for contraband to be landed somewhere along the shore of Christchurch Bay, west of Lymington. Richard Perrin from Chichester went to Guernsey as buyer, and purchased 27 bags of tea (almost 42 cwt) and 30 casks of brandy, which cost about £500. Richard Perrin, who was later to die at Tyburn for his part in the affair, was probably a victim of circumstance. He had been an honest carpenter until illness robbed him of the use of a hand; at 36 he was one of the oldest men to take part. The cutter *Three Brothers* carrying the tea and brandy left Guernsey in September 1747, but was seen and captured by a Revenue vessel under Captain Johnson, taken into Poole, and its cargo held in the Custom House there. The crew had escaped overboard into a small boat, and Richard Perrin went back to Hawkhurst to explain what had happened. Ten days later a large group of smugglers from the Chichester area, and Richard Perrin as representative of the Hawkhurst Gang, met in Charlton Forest to plan the rescue of what all regarded as 'their' property. The participants put their mark to an agreement undertaking to support one another in riding as an armed convoy to Poole to seize the cargo. The following night 23 of these men met at Rowland's Castle with their horses and arms, and were joined by Thomas Kingsmill and six other men from Hawkhurst as they waited for darkness in the Forest of Bere. That night they rode some twenty-five miles to Lyndhurst in the New Forest, where they rested. The following evening the convoy rode on, to reach the outskirts of Poole by 11 p.m. Two men then went forward to reconnoitre, and returned with the unwelcome news that a sloop-of-war was moored alongside the quay, with guns able to command any attack on the Custom House. A further conference took place, and the more ruthless Hawkhurst men declared that if necessary they alone would break in and seize the goods. It was then realised that as the tide fell, the warship's guns could no longer be fired onto the quay, so the smugglers rode down a backlane on the east side of Poole, taking with them a youth they encountered, lest he raise the alarm. The horses were left with the handicapped Richard Perrin and the youngest member of the party, Thomas Lillywhite. They 141

Bosham in Chichester Harbour. Once the outport for Chichester, Bosham was used regularly by smugglers.

broke into the Custom House with axes and crowbars and carried off the tea, but – surprisingly – left the brandy behind. Having loaded the horses, they set off north along a route regularly used by Dorset smugglers, riding straight through Fordingbridge. Near Brook in the New Forest they stopped to weigh out the tea and ensure that each man received his rightful share (about 135 lbs) at the successful conclusion of the enterprise.

Significantly there is no mention in any contemporary version of this story that the gang met the slightest opposition either in Poole or on their extensive travels. But for one exuberant gesture they might all have remained undetected. As the convoy passed through Fordingbridge, among the many people watching was a certain shoemaker called Daniel Chater. He recognised the smuggler John Diamond; they talked briefly, and Diamond gave Chater a bag of tea 'for old times' sake'. It was to seal the fate of both men.

Once the authorities realised the significance of the raid on Poole, a reward of £500 was offered for information leading to the capture of those responsible. Daniel Chater did not immediately betray his

142

acquaintance, but he boasted about what had happened. As a conse
quence Diamond was arrested and held in Chichester gaol. It was
then necessary for Daniel Chater to identify Diamond before JP
Major Battine of East Marden near Chichester. Accordingly Chater
was provided with an escort, William Galley, an elderly man employed in the Customs service to rummage vessels. On the 14th of
February 1748 the two men set off on specially hired horses and in
their Sunday best, to ride from Southampton to Major Battine's
house. East Marden village, where Battine lived, is not very easily
accessible today; in the eighteenth century it could probably have
been most conveniently reached along the old road from Winchester
(now mainly unmetalled tracks), which ran through Clanfield, Chal-
ton, Chilgrove and West Dean. Galley and Chater, however, set off
along the coast road through Havant. So two inexperienced and
unarmed men rode straight into the heart of smuggler country on
their way to lay information against an important gang member.
They stopped for refreshment and to ask the way, and presently found
themselves in the White Hart Inn at Rowlands Castle. The landlady
sent for two notorious local smugglers, William Jackson and William
Carter, who soon discovered the purpose of Chater's journey. The
shoemaker and his escort were now doomed, since Galley's information could bring all those involved at Poole to the gallows. As a first
step Galley and Chater were rendered befuddled by drink, while the
smugglers discussed what to do. They were then dragged outside,
beaten and tortured and each was tied onto a horse. The smugglers
next rode with their victims along one of their regular routes inland,
up the valley north of Rowland's Castle through Finchdean to Old
Idsworth Farm, and then along what is now a footpath, through the
park of Lady Holt House. The smugglers evidently intended to throw
William Galley's body down a well in the park. However, despite his
injuries, Galley was not yet dead, so they continued over Harting
Down, across the Rother Valley and Rogate Common to reach the
Red Lion Inn at Rake (on what is now the A3) by the early hours of
next morning. The Red Lion was evidently a safe house and regular
stopping place on the route to London, but the landlord must have
been too horrified by the condition of the dying Galley to admit them.
They retreated about a mile southwards, and Galley was buried
(perhaps still alive) in a foxearth at Harting Combe, where his body
was discovered seven months later.

Daniel Chater's sufferings were more prolonged. He was chained in
an outhouse at Trotton, beside the home of another smuggling household, Richard Mills and his son. He was finally killed by being thrown
into a well in Lady Holt Park and stoned to death.

The perpetrators of this hideous violence were not members of the   143

Hawkhurst Gang but belonged to the associated group based around Chichester. In mitigation of their bestial behaviour it can be said that they were certainly drunk, and probably egged on by their wives. Their aim was to intimidate any potential informer. At this time the names of known smugglers were published in the London Gazette; if thereafter these men failed to surrender within forty days, they automatically faced the death penalty, and £500 was offered for information leading to the arrest of any gazetted smuggler. In November 1748, 103 names were published. The Hampshire smugglers William Carter and William Jackson from Rowland's Castle were on this list, with John Broad of Upper Leigh, Havant. Many of the Hawkhurst Gang were also named: Jeremiah Curtis (otherwise William Pollard), Jeremiah Creed, Thomas Dixon (Shoemaker Tom) and Thomas Buffis (Pouncer) all of Hawkhurst, and Thomas Cheeseman (Butcher Tom) of Wadhurst, Thomas Winter (Footsey) from near Ashford, Jacob Pring from Beckenham, fifteen other men from the Folkestone and Ashford areas of Kent, three from Sittingbourne and two from Bexhill. All these men lived in constant fear of betrayal and in consequence could act with exceptional brutality against any potential informer. A few months earlier Richard Hawkins, a young labourer suspected of stealing two bags of tea from a cache near Yapton, was beaten to death in the Dog and Partridge Inn on Slindon Common nearby. Apparently the gang had miscounted, and Richard Hawkins was an innocent victim; Jeremiah Curtis and John Mills (whose father lived at Trotton) were later judged to have killed him. So effectively was the local population intimidated that when in August 1748 thirteen smugglers (including Curtis, Fairall and Kingsmill from Hawkhurst) carried out a major robbery at the home of the owner of the George Inn at Petersfield, he dare not report his losses until most of those involved were safely in gaol.

The first Hawkhurst man to turn king's evidence was Jacob Pring of Beckenham. Already an outlaw and gazetted smuggler, Pring decided to betray some of his companions, and even to engineer their capture. He rode to Bristol, and persuaded John Mills and the brothers Thomas and Lawrence Kemp to return with him to Beckenham, where he entertained them in his home. Using the excuse that he had to obtain fresh horses for a planned highway robbery, Pring then rode to Horsham to inform the local Excise officer and returned with sufficient men to arrest the three Hawkhurst villains. Jacob Pring had also been with the raiding party to Poole, so presently the names of other participants leaked out. Two of these, William Steele and John Race, also turned informer. William Steele disclosed the names of some 26 men who went to Poole, seven of whom were involved in the murders of Galley and Chater. His deposition was sent

The seaward end of South Street; Emsworth, once notorious for smuggling.

to Prime Minister Henry Pelham. The bestial savagery of these disclosures outraged contemporary society, and a determined effort was made to round up all those involved. In the trials which followed, Thomas Kingsmill, William Fairall and Richard Perrin were convicted at the Old Bailey and hanged at Tyburn (Fairall's body was then gibbeted where he had lived at Horsemonden in Kent, and Kingsmill's at Goudhurst). Four more of the Hawkhurst gang were tried at Rochester and hanged on Penenden Heath outside Maidstone. Eight others died for their parts in the murder of Thomas Carswell near Battle and Michael Bath at Sea Place, Goring, as well as other crimes. Six out of seven men tried at East Grinstead for the murder of Richard Hawkins and other crimes were hanged (the seventh was transported).

In January 1749 a Special Assize was held at Chichester to deal with the murders of Galley and Chater. The justices travelled from London over Hind Heath to Midhurst and Chichester in six coaches, each drawn by six horses. The Duke of Richmond met the party in Midhurst and entertained them in his hunting lodge in Charlton Forest. The trial itself was an occasion of great solemnity and ceremony. The evidence was written down by 'a Gentleman of Chichester' (very probably the Duke of Richmond himself) and subsequently 145 published as *A Full and Genuine History of the Inhuman and Unparalleled Murders of Mr William Galley, a custom-house officer, and Mr Daniel Chater.* ... The seven men on trial were all judged guilty of the murders and were condemned. William Jackson died in prison the night before the others were hanged on the Broyle outside Chichester. An inscribed stone, now supplemented by a more readable notice, marks the spot. Subsequently the body of Benjamin Tapner, who murdered Chater, was hung in chains on St Roches Hill, beside the Trundle, until that gibbet was destroyed by lightning. John Cobby and John Hammond, labourers from the Bognor area and also guilty of Chater's murder, were gibbeted on Selsey Bill, where they commonly smuggled. The body of William Carter, murderer of Galley, was gibbeted at Rake on the Portsmouth Road. Richard Mills and his son, both of Trotton and accessories to the murder of Chater, were buried on the Broyle.

Two Hampshire smugglers also implicated in these crimes, were also captured. The Riding Officers of Cosham, Fareham and Titchfield caught Richard Broad of Hambledon, and three months later, John Broad of Upper Leigh, Havant was taken by an officer at Emsworth. Among the Goodwood papers at Chichester is the Duke's own list of smugglers apprehended and executed. In less than three years he was able to record that 45 had died (eight in gaol and one by drowning, but the rest were executed). Of the Hawkhurst leaders only Jeremiah Curtis (otherwise Alexander Pollard) appears to have escaped by living abroad.

One of the minor characters in the story deserves special mention. Thomas Lillywhite, a lad of barely 17 from near Storrington, had ridden with the party to Poole, where he had held the horses but taken no part in any violence. Sir Cecil Bishop of Parham House appealed for mercy to be shown him, but the Duke of Richmond was adamant that he was as guilty as the rest, and indeed Thomas Lillywhite was already known to the gang as Slotch and could hardly claim ignorance of what was going on. His own beautifully written letter from Horsham gaol, in which he appeals for his life and speaks of 'my boyish youth' and signs himself 'your unhappy and dutiful servant', can still be seen in West Sussex Record Office. Rather surprisingly he was acquitted and went on to found a law-abiding family; among his direct descendents were the famous cricketers.

After 1749 and the death of many gang leaders, lower Customs duties reduced the profitability of smuggling. The trade continued, but in routine fashion and on a reduced scale. It was not until about 1780, with the re-imposition of high tarrifs, that smuggling again became a major industry in the Chichester area. On land this was actively opposed by Mr Walter's men, and his subordinate Mr Hubbard was injured in a typical fight at Eartham (near Chichester) in 1788. In that year and again in 1706, soldiers from the garrison at Port Cumberland outside Portsmouth helped with the capture of smugglers. The scale of operations at this time may be gauged from the sale of 12,372 gallons of spirits captured at Selsey in 1789. At a time when many officials were bribed or intimidated in turning a blind eye to what went on, the courage of Thomas Gloge, Revenue Boatman at Hayling Island, deserves mention. In 1788 he and three other officers were captured by smugglers during a running fight in Langstone Harbour. When attempts to buy their silence failed, they were held captive overnight at Bedhampton, until Thomas Gloge escaped to raise the alarm. Four years later another attempt was made. Gloge was unsuccessfully offered £50, through an intermediary, by James Hunt, landlord of the Pack Horse Inn at Stansted. Hunt himself was then living at Southsea Castle, where the cellars were found to contain almost a thousand casks of contraband spirits. Stansted lay on one of the regular routes used to transport goods inland. Racton Tower, a folly in Stansted Park, is thought to have been used for signalling. Westbourne (where there is still a smuggler's cottage north of the church) and Rowland's Castle remained important centres. There was storage in Chichester itself, and Brandy Hole Lane on the north west outskirts commemorates this. During the building of the College of Education, workmen discovered a tunnel leading in the direction of the sea.

Along the West Sussex and Solent coasts it was the large well-armed smuggling cutters which posed such problems in the 1780s. Fast vessels of 200 tons and more, carrying armed men and twenty guns were more than a match for the few Revenue vessels then on patrol. The cutter *Richmond* had been stationed in Chichester Harbour in 1753, and over the following thirty years the number and size of Revenue vessels had been increased. Naval vessels from Portsmouth also gave assistance from time to time, but of these only the *Orestes*, a warship of 300 tons with 18 guns, then patrolling the Dorset coast, was really adequate to the task. Chichester Harbour was then being patrolled by the *Roebuck*, a much smaller Revenue vessel. In May 1784 her captain reported that when he tried to arrest one cutter bringing in contraband, another came up, and he was forced to assume the role of helpless spectator. In an attempt to supplement the Revenue craft, the government encouraged private individuals to build and equip vessels capable of challenging the smugglers, the incentive being prize-money for a successful venture. One man already dedicated to eradicating the trade and willing to take up this opportunity was William Arnold (whose son later became the famous headmaster of Rugby School). Arnold had been appointed Collector   147

A contemporary print showing William Galley (1) and Daniel Chater (2) tied together on horseback after being seized by smugglers at Rowlands Castle.

of Customs at Cowes on the Isle of Wight in 1777, and from then until his death in 1801, he struggled vigorously to prevent the running of contraband. In 1783 he built and equipped his own vessel, the *Swan*, which sailed under Captain Sarmon. A month later, while looking for smugglers, his uninsured ship was disastrously wrecked on Hurst Castle Spit near Lymington. Fortunately the authorities decided to replace Arnold's vessel, so *Swan II* was built and based at Cowes from 1784 until she too was wrecked on the West Sussex coast while chasing a Hastings smuggler, in 1792. *Swan II* was involved in two particular episodes off the Sussex coast. In December 1790 the Revenue cutter *Rose* had been patrolling off Beachy Head when she was fired on by a larger and better armed smuggling vessel. Prudently the *Rose* withdrew, but the next night *Swan II* arrived to find goods still being run ashore. The smugglers promptly commandeered the *Swan*'s small boat and held its crew prisoner while the landing continued. (The smugglers were from Guernsey and had blackened their faces with gunpowder.) When all the contraband was ashore, the *Swan*'s boat and crew were released – and given two small tubs in payment! A month later the honour of *Swan II* was redeemed; her crew captured a fine new 200 ton vessel belonging to smuggler James Winhorne of Hastings. She was taken into government service, renamed the *Greyhound*, and as the largest vessel in the Revenue fleet, went on to patrol the Channel between Start Point, Devon and Beachy Head.

In 1793 England and France were again at war, and the revenue vessels had to face French privateers as well as smuggling craft. Both *Swan III* and *Swan IV*, successively based at Cowes between 1793 and 1797, were captured by the French. When at last after twenty-two years of almost continuous warfare with France, the men of West Sussex came back to their homes, many were forced by the lack of adequate employment to become part-time smugglers once more. These coasts were never as effectively guarded as those further east, and the more determined smugglers from Kent and East Sussex sought to continue their trade in the quiet backwaters of Pagham and Chichester Harbours. Despite outspoken criticism by the vicar of Walberton, the local people still gave their support to the smugglers. When a butcher informed against John Reeves, the miller at Selsey, the villagers attacked his home, and burned him in effigy. Though there were still fights with the Revenue men (in the cellars of the Crown and Anchor Inn at Dell Quay according to legend), secrecy and guile were the order of the day. Years later, Joseph Robinson of Pagham was to recall with satisfaction the night in 1830 when over a thousand pound's worth of liquor was run into Pagham Harbour by galley. Other recognised methods included bringing in the goods beneath a catch of oysters, or towing a raft of tubs behind or under-

149

neath a vessel. In 1837 a strange craft was washed ashore near Selsey Bill. This crude wooden boat had holes in the keel so that a cargo of tubs (held in by a net) would stay below the waterline while the whole contraption was being towed. The story is also told of a fine hearse and funeral cortege meeting a vessel which came into Chichester Harbour with her flag at half mast. The 'body' was reverently taken ashore, but the hearse then set off at high speed!

Smuggling by means of various deceptions continued for many years, and the Coastguard records of the 1840s and 1850s list numerous seizures of spirits and tobacco. In 1849, for example, tubs were captured on Cockbush Common, West Wittering, and the same year a steam tug impudently towed a raft of contraband into Portsmouth Harbour. Tobacco smuggling, in particular, continued into the 1870s.

PLACES TO VISIT

Two Short Walks
Emsworth to Langstone   (2 miles)
Carpark in South Street, Emsworth. South Street leads directly from the quay back to the Square. Some fine buildings in the streets opening off this square are an indication of the town's prosperity as outport for Chichester, with important ship building and oyster fishing industries. It also became a minor watering place, patronised by royalty. At high tide the sea laps against the back walls of houses and gardens; contraband could be ferried in directly or sunk offshore to await recovery by a vessel ostensibly oyster fishing. Much came ashore near the church on Thorney Island. A tunnel from the summer house on the harbour wall behind Trentham House led to cellars below The Old Pharmacy in King Street. (Workmen servicing a water main found the tunnel, and a narrow staircase led up to a hideout on the roof.)

From the seaward end of South Street walk westwards along the embanked millpond of a former tide mill, and then by a signed field path to Langstone, passing Warblington Church and castle ruins. The path passes Langstone Mill, known to have been regularly used for storage, and leads to the Royal Oak Inn at the foot of Langstone High Street, a meeting place for the local smuggling community. The old causeway can be seen leading across to Hayling Island.

Pagham Harbour, Sidlesham and Church Norton
Parking on the B2145 at SZ 857964 (where the former ferry linked Sidlesham to Selsey). A thousand acres in and around Pagham Harbour now form a nature reserve managed by West Sussex Coun-

oil. An information centre and nature trail provide a guide to the most interesting features. Pagham Harbour was once known as Selsey Haven, and shipping came up to the quay at Sidlesham until silting blocked the navigable channel. (An unsuccessful attempt was made to reclaim the whole area for farming between 1873 and 1910.) Joseph Robinson, whose reminiscences are preserved in West Sussex Record Office, was born at Pagham in 1820. He recalled one profitable run in 1830 when about 700 tubs, worth over £1100 were brought in by a galley which made use of a following spring tide. The Revenuemen had been lured away by a light in mill creek at Sidlesham.

One can walk northwards to Sidlesham Quay, or along the harbour shore to Church Norton. The small church there is only the remnant of the medieval structure; most of the building was moved to a new site in Selsey itself in 1866. It is known that there was a tunnel leading to the old rectory beyond the church. Much of the smuggling took place nearer to Selsey Bill, but modern development has effectively submerged most links with this past.

Other Visits and View Points

East Head, West Wittering
Extensive car parking (charge) along the coast, with cafe and toilets, at SZ 772979, approached by a road from near East Wittering church. A considerable stretch of unspoilt coast where many cargoes were landed. East Head, a shifting spit of sand dunes and marram grass, is now under the protection of the National Trust, and there is a nature trail here. Excellent views towards the Isle of Wight and over Chichester Harbour and Hayling Island. For those who wish to explore further, the path along the Chichester Harbour shore to Itchenor leaves from the north-western corner of the carpark, and passes the former Coastguard cottages.

St Roches Hill, beside The Trundle
Parking at SU 872110 immediately west of the Trundle and Good-wood Race Course. The approach (unsigned and narrow) is from the north, where the minor road coming up from Singleton turns sharply left (east) towards the race course. The old road from Chichester to Midhurst is now a track which comes up from East Lavant to this spot, and continued down to Singleton. The body of Hawkhurst smuggler Benjamin Tapner was hung in chains here in 1749. The view south to the Isle of Wight over Chichester and its branching harbour is excellent. There is also the opportunity to climb up the Trundle, where the summit is ringed by an Iron Age entrenchment and a much older Neolithic causewayed camp.

151

Postscript

It was the reduction of Customs duties after 1840 which took much of the profit out of smuggling and this, coupled with the vigilance of the Coastguard service, effectively stopped large scale operations for the next hundred years. Smaller enterprises continued, particularly on our remoter coasts. The Cornish miners were kept supplied with spirits and tobacco, mainly from Brittany and brought ashore in local Coves. At the other end of England, the 'Boomer men' from Boulmer in Northumberland, ferried in supplies to supplement illicit liquor distilled in valleys along the Scottish border. At all times Ireland acted as intermediary through which uncustomed tobacco reached our western coasts, and in an attempt to revive old practices two men tried unsuccessfully to bring a cargo of brandy ashore at Cuckmere Haven in 1923.

The period of shortages after the Second World War and the availability of suitable war surplus craft revived interest in the trade. The *Taku*, a former air-sea rescue craft, was caught with a cargo of spirits in Poole Harbour in 1947. The *Dawn Approach* was intercepted at Beaumaris in Anglesey with a cargo of Swiss watches in 1951 (after making at least twenty successful voyages). Indeed it is thought that half the Swiss watches entering the country at this time were smuggled; I still have the one I bought from an Oxford Street trader! Instances of individual enterprise continued during the 1960s: a fishing boat laden with spirits and tobacco was seized off Teignmouth in Devon in 1964. Other captures included a yacht which put into Margate carrying Dutch cigars in 1967, and an ex-Custom House launch caught with more cigars in Faversham creek in 1969. A more widespread traffic along the south east coast at this time concerned the arrival of illegal immigrants, brought ashore in Sandwich Bay, on Romney Marsh and at Cuckmere Haven among other places. It is believed that in the five years following the tightening of immigration control, some 50,000 were brought in at the going rate of between £50 and £100 a head.

A new and far more sinister aspect of smuggling developed as organised crime moved into the lucrative drugs traffic after 1970. The expansion of cargo carrying by air and container lorry created quite new opportunities. By 1982 Dover alone was handling 5,000,000 container lorries a year. Increasingly sophisticated surveillance tech-

liquor can hardly be expected to match this spectacular expansion.
Smuggling is once again a major British industry, with consequences
potentially far more serious now than they were two centuries ago.
Though many features of the trade are quite new, others have interesting historical parallels. Where earlier operations sought to protect
the cloth trade by banning the export of wool, we aim to keep the
secrets of high technology. For example during 1983 the shipping out
of American computer equipment through Poole, Sheerness and
Dover was stopped. The transfer of 'hot' money into numbered Swiss
bank accounts or its conversion into Krugerrands for more convenient handling is the modern equivalent of the guinea smuggling of
Napoleonic times.

The detail of some of the more important recent seizures shows a
telling amalgam of well established custom and modern innovation.
Thus the 'Race Horse Set' began running drugs from North Africa to
Torbay in 1975, but then (following the precedent of earlier Devon
smugglers) moved operations to the remote beach at Talland Bay
near Looe, where they created an underground store beneath the cafe,
now appropriately known as the Smugglers' Rest. They brought in
cannabis, using the converted trawler *Guiding Lights*, and are believed
to have amassed £40,000,000 in Swiss and other banks or 'laundered'
through Gibraltar. In 1979 the forty-strong reception committee of
'Operation Cyril' watched by moonlight as they brought a further 2½
tons of cannabis ashore in a rubber dinghy, and the same night other
officers raided the gang's London depot in Penge. At the Old Bailey
trial which followed, thirteen men from 'good' addresses in the Home
Counties and Cheshire were duly convicted. In March 1981 the
Panamanian vessel *Sea Rover* was chased across the Channel by both
French and British Customs cutters, and her cargo was jettisoned.
She was boarded off Beachy Head and taken to Newhaven, where
fragments of burnt cannabis were found aboard. Other seizures of
cannabis at this time included fifteen tons (worth about £20,000,000)
on the Scottish island of Kerera, off Oban.

The heroin traffic is more sinister still. During 1982 heroin with a
street value of £28,000,000 was seized in Britain, and the following
year East Sussex police alone seized £2,500,000 worth of the drug.
Heroin is now said to be cheaper on the streets of Hastings than
anywhere else in the country. The traffic may be coming in through
Rye Harbour, where the Custom House (whose windows face inland)
works office hours. In March 1984 the battered body of a young
Hastings drug dealer was found in woods at nearby Brightling, where
it is thought he cached his stock. Investigation of this case continues.

In July 1984 heroin, said to be worth £6,000,000, was brought
ashore on a North Wales beach, where the gang, which included a   153

London businessman, had a specially constructed hide. The following September there was a different type of operation. A vessel running guns for the IRA from the United States was shadowed by spy satelite and arrested off the south west coast of Ireland. A month later the startled residents of a small village on the river Crouch in Essex found themselves at the heart of an SAS type operation. The vessel *Robert Gordon* was caught with six tons of top quality Lebanese cannabis on board, worth over £7,000,000. In December 1984 Pakistani heroin worth £2,500,000 was discovered in a motor caravan at Dover Hoverport, the largest seizure of this type so far.

So what of the future, and what of our attitude to smuggler and preventiveman down the years?

KEY DATES IN THE SMUGGLING STORY

1690 French victory in a battle off Beachy Head

1698 Act against owling creates a landguard of Riding Officers
Rigid controls imposed on buying and selling wool within 15 miles of the coast

1702–12 War of the Spanish Succession

1706 Act of Union between England and Scotland

1715 Rebellion in Scotland under the Old Pretender

1717 Smuggling Act. Smugglers who refused to plead liable to transportation

1718 Hovering Act. Vessels under 50 tons liable to seizure if found loitering within 6 miles of the coast, and liable to seizure if laden with tea, brandy, silk etc

1721 Smuggling Act. Convicted smugglers to be transported for 7 years. Boats with more than 4 oars liable to confiscation and destruction

1724 Robert Walpole adds tea to items liable to Excise duty and creates bonded warehouses.

1725 Robert Walpole increases the Excise on malt

1729 Increased duties on cheap spirits

1733 Robert Walpole tries unsuccessfully to extend Excise duty to tobacco

1736 Inquiry under Sir John Cope takes evidence on smuggling
Smuggling Act increases penalties; severe fines for bribing officers, death for wounding or taking up arms against officers, transportation (if unarmed) for resisting arrest. Also an Act of Indemnity; a smuggler, even if in gaol, could have a free pardon if he confessed all and gave names of his associates

1739 War of Jenkin's Ear (with Spain and related to smuggling in the West Indies)

1740–48 War of Austrian Succession (a serious drain on the Exchequer)

1744 Threat of invasion from France

1745 Rebellion under Bonnie Prince Charlie, the Young Pretender. Parliamentary Inquiry into the tea trade. Tea duty cut by Henry Pelham
Further penalties for those found loitering within 6 miles of coast

1746 Battle of Culloden and final defeat of the Jacobite cause
Smuggling Act established the severest penalties, initially for a
7 year period. Death for running contraband, assembling to run
goods or harbouring smugglers. Smugglers convicted of killing
officers were to be gibbeted. Collective fines on whole county for
unresolved offences (£100 for an officer killed by smugglers, £40
for one wounded). Names of known smugglers published in the
London Gazette; these men to surrender within 40 days or be
judged guilty. £500 reward for anyone turning in a gazetted
smuggler

1749 The Special Assize at Chichester to try the murderers of Galley
and Chater. The breakup of the major gangs of Kent and
Sussex

1751 Further controls on the trade in gin and tobacco

1756–63 Seven Years War, involving fighting in India, Africa, North
America and Europe

1759 Tea duty raised again

1765 Isle of Man brought within Customs control

1767 First attempt to establish a Custom House in Jersey

1775–83 War of American Independence

1779 Smuggling Act, amending measures of 1746 Act and adding
penalties for goods carried in vessels under 200 tons. Boats with
more than 4 oars forbidden. Penalties for gaolers allowing
smugglers to escape

1782 Act of Oblivion. Smugglers could redeem their crimes by finding men to serve in army and navy. One landsman and one
seaman could compound a £500 penalty, and two of each could
redeem *all* penalties, however great

1783 Report of the Commission of Excise on Smuggling

1784 The Younger Pitt, as Prime Minister, cuts tea duty from 127%
to 12½% but increases Window Tax. Further modifications to
Smuggling and Hovering Acts. Prohibition on building certain
types of boats

1793–1815 War with France, the Revolutionary and Napoleonic
Wars, interrupted by short interval of peace March 1802 – May
1803

1795 Chain of signal stations link the south east coast to London

1797 Naval mutinies at Spithead and the Nore

1805 Customs control extended to the Channel Isles

1806 Start of construction of Martello towers and Royal Military
Canal

1809 New Preventive Waterguard created

1815 First rocket lifesaving apparatus tried out

156 1816 Control of Revenue cutters transferred to Admiralty

1817 Coast Blockade initially established between North and South Forelands

1818 Coast Blockade extended to cover coast from Sheerness to Seaford

1822 National Coast Guard established on other coasts; further extension of Coast Blockade into West Sussex

1826 Further modifications to Smuggling Acts

1828 Customs control extended to the Scilly Isles

1830 Rural unrest in Kent and Sussex culminates in the Swing Riots

1831 Coastguard service replaces Coast Blockade in Kent and Sussex

1835 First steamer employed in the Preventive service

1839 Commission of Inquiry into the Coastguard service

1844 Select Committee Report on the Tobacco Trade

1845 Sir Robert Peel removes duties on a wide range of items

1846 Repeal of the Corn Laws

1850 Last export duty (on coal in foreign ships) abolished

1853 Gladstone reforms the Customs service

Appendix 2

LEADING MEMBERS OF THE MAYFIELD, GROOMBRIDGE AND HAWKHURST GANGS

These lists (inevitably incomplete) are based on the names and nicknames which appear in the Goodwood and Sayer manuscripts, and the research by Paul Muskett. There are problems and uncertainties because of handwriting and spelling!

THE MAYFIELD GANG

Leader *Gabriel Tomkins*, otherwise Kitt Jarvis, Unkle, Joseph Rawlins. A bricklayer from Tunbridge Wells who led successful owling operations before 1717. Suspecting of murdering an officer near Eastbourne in 1717 but acquitted. Jan 1721 involved with Excisemen at Reigate. March 1721 shot in the arm while escaping at Lydd. Sept 1721 captured at Nutley. Sentenced to transportation, but talked his way to freedom. Smuggling again in 1728/9, recaptured, and in 1733 gave evidence to Sir John Cope's inquiry. Appointed a Riding Officer, and by 1735 Customs Officer at Dartford and Bailiff to Sheriff of Sussex; involved in episode at Rye. Fled from Dartford in 1741. Robbed Chester Mail 1746. Tried and hanged at Bedford 1750, for highway robbery.

Other Members:

Thomas Bigg   Involved in the escape at Lydd in 1721.

Francis Hammond   Arrested at Mayfield but soon released by the Tomkins brothers

John Humphrey

Francis Norwood

Alexander Pain

Edward Tomkins, otherwise Jarvis, half brother of Gabriel. Captured a Customs officer while running brandy at Seaford in 1721. Was himself captured several times by John Rogers, but freed by the magistrate.

Jacob Walters   Captured but escaped at Lydd in 1721; was working with Gabriel Tomkins in 1728/9. Finally captured by Lieut. Burnett near Battle and tried in London.

William Weller

The gang broke up as a result of Gabriel Tomkins' capture in 1721, but some members apparently transferred activities to the Horsham area.

Wimble, who ran an inn at Bulverhythe (The Bull?) worked with the gang.

THE GROOMBRIDGE GANG or Moreton's People

Leaders *John Bowra*, known to have built a fine house in Groombridge. Tried in 1737 but apparently acquitted.
Robert Moreton of Groombridge led the gang until 1749.

Other Members:
John Barbar 'late of Bodiam'.
Thomas Bridger of Groombridge.
Thomas Gurr of Groombridge, known as Stick-in-the-mud.
John Kitchen known as Flushing Jack.
Thomas Nokes of Great Cockham, Kent (Crockham Hill?)
Richard Ovenden 'late of Westerham'.
Robert Parmer or *Farmer* of Groombridge
Isaac Pope of Groombridge, known as Towzer.
Robert Pope of Hartfield.
Thomas Ward of Groombridge, known as Bulverhythe Tom.
William Weston of Rotherfield, arrested 1736 but escaped.

Other unidentified nicknames:
Old Joll, Toll, The Miller, Yorkshire George and Nasty Face.
Jerome Knapp (former gang member?) provided most of these names for the trial at Rochester in December 1749.
James Blackman, innkeeper at what is now the Red Lion at Hooe, near Pevensey, worked with the gang.

THE HAWKHURST GANG

Leader until 1747: *Arthur Gray*, built Gray's Folly on Seacox Heath and said to be worth £10,000. Indicted for highway robbery and murder of Thomas Carswell in 1744. Hanged 1748.
Leader from 1747: *Thomas Kingsmill*, native of Goudhurst. Numerous crimes for which he was hanged at Tyburn and gibbeted at Goudhurst.

Other Members:
John Amos of Robertsbridge.
John Boxall, who later turned King's evidence and betrayed many members.
Thomas Buffis of Hawkhurst, known as Pouncer.
George Chapman of Hurst Green, gibbeted at Hurst Green for murder of Carswell.
Thomas Cheeseman of Wadhurst, known as Butcher Tom.
Jeremiah (or Uriah) Creed of Hawkhurst.
Jeremiah Curtis, otherwise Alexander Pollard or Butler. Initially one of 'The Transports' gang but later a key member of Hawkhurst gang.   159

Indicted for various crimes, including murder of Richard Hawkins. Apparently escaped justice by going to live in France.

Thomas Dixon known as Shoemaker Tom.

Thomas Dury of Benenden.

William Dury of Flimwell.

William Fairall of Horsemonden. One of the leaders of the Poole episode. Hanged at Tyburn and gibbeted at Horsemonden.

William Gray, brother of Arthur Gray. Built a house at Goudhurst. Captured by the Cranbrook Association in 1747. Either transported or died in gaol.

George Kingsmill, brother of Thomas Kingsmill. Killed at Goudhurst, 1747.

Thomas Kingswood of Flimwell.

John Munton of Hawkhurst 'late of Sittingbourne'.

William Potter of Benenden, captured by the Cranbrook Association, 1747.

Jacob Pring or *Prim* of Beckenham. Turned King's evidence.

James Stanford, otherwise Trip, of Monksfield. An important and wealthy member.

Thomas Trowell of Hawkhurst.

John Waite (of Earsfield?).

David Wenham of Hurst Green, probably known as Old Oatmeal.

Thomas Winter of Postling, Kent, known as Footsey.

Smugglers from Chichester area, known to have worked with Hawkhurst men:

William Carter of Rowlands Castle. Tried and hanged at Chichester, gibbeted at Rake.

John Cobby of Bognor. Tried at Chichester and gibbeted at Selsey Bill.

John Diamond or *Dimer*, born in Dorset. Tried and hanged at Chichester.

John Hammond of Bognor. Tried at Chichester and gibbeted at Selsey Bill.

William Jackson of Rowlands Castle. Tried at Chichester and died in prison.

Lawrence Kemp betrayed by Jacob Pring.

Thomas Kemp betrayed by Jacob Pring.

John Mills of Trotton, son of Richard Mills. Hanged at Chichester as accessory to murder of Chater and murderer of Richard Hawkins. Gibbeted at Slindon.

Richard Mills of Trotton, hanged as accessory to murder of Chater.

Richard Perrin of Chichester, former carpenter and purchaser of tea seized at Poole. Hanged at Tyburn.

John Race who was at Poole but turned King's evidence.

William Steele who was at Poole but turned King's evidence.

Benjamin Tapner, hanged for murder of Chater and gibbeted on St Roches Hill

Thomas Lillewhite (who was a schoolboy). Admitted being at Rowe but finally acquitted following various appeals, because of his age.

Other Known Associates of the Hawkhurst Gang:

John Grayling of the Hastings Outlaws or The Transports. Sentenced to 7 years transportation in 1738.

Thomas Holman, a relative of John Collier, who appealed on his behalf. Finally sentenced to transportation, but went to live in France.

Larry Jockey of 'Horse Mountsey' (Herstmonceux).

Edward Savage of Bexhill.

John Turner, landlord of the inn at Whatlington, known as Cursemother Jack.

Unidentified nicknames include Rough Tickner and Poison.

Appendix 3

GLOSSARY

Anker: A measure of spirits, roughly 7½ gallons; half anker 3½ to 4 gallons.

Bat: A long wooden stave used as a weapon by smugglers.

Boatsitter: A chief boatman in the Preventive Waterguard.

Coast Blockade: The preventive system in Kent and Sussex, 1817–31.

Coastguard: (first called the Coast Guard) The national preventive service established under Capt W Bowles, appointed 1822.

Coastwaiter: The Customs officer responsible for vessels from home ports.

Collector: The head of the Customs personnel at each port.

Comptroller: The Collector's deputy at the larger ports.

Cutter: A single-masted vessel, rigged like a sloop but with a running bowsprit.

Dragoon: A mounted soldier.

Exciseman: An officer responsible for assessing and collecting Excise Duty.

Flink Pistol: Used to flash a signal; in appearance like a starting gun.

Free trader: A smuggler.

Galley: A large open rowboat, typically propelled by up to 20 oars.

Gauger: An Exciseman responsible for measuring spirits and calculating duty.

Geneva: Gin, also known as Hollands.

Hanger: A sword.

Jacobite: A supporter of James II after his abdication, or of his son.

Landwaiter: The Customs official who supervised the unloading of ships from foreign ports.

Lugger: A vessel with four-cornered sails, rigged fore-and-aft.

Militia: A military unit, sometimes a volunteer unit. Mainly established under Acts of 1757–8, when men were chosen to serve by ballot, but substitutes were allowed.

Owler: Anyone smuggling wool out of England.

Preventive Waterguard: Preventive service established in 1809 covering whole country in 3 districts; patrols by cutters and small preventive boats.

Privateer: A privately-owned armed vessel holding a government commission (Letters of Marque) to wage war on enemy ships.

Riding Officer: Officer in the Customs service appointed to patrol on
horseback, initially to counter the owling trade.

Run: A successful landing of contraband.

Safe House: An inn or other building providing a recognised refuge
for smugglers, usually with storage and stabling.

Sloop: or Shallop. A small single-masted, fore-and-aft rigged ship.

Sowing a crop: Sinking a raft of tubs in a marked position offshore.

Spout lantern: A signalling lantern made to send out a beam of light
through a long spout attachment.

Tap: An unlicenced beer house.

Tide Surveyor: The Customs officer responsible for rummaging
(searching) vessels anchored in port.

Tub: A wooden cask holding a ½ anker of spirits (3½–4 gallons);
often roped in pairs to be carried over the shoulder.

Whig: (originally) A member of the political party which supported
the revolution of 1688; the party led by Sir Robert Walpole.

Bibliography

The most important contemporary source on smuggling between 1720 and 1750 is the correspondence of John Collier, hereafter referred to as the *Sayer Manuscripts*. The original letters are in East Sussex Record Office, and transcriptions can be seen there and in Kent County Record Office. John Collier (1685–1760) was a solicitor who held office as Mayor of Hastings, Baron of the Cinque Ports and Surveyor-General of Riding Officers in Kent, and was appointed to manage the Sussex estates of the Pelham family. Over 2000 letters survive, the earliest dating from 1716. The correspondence of the Duke of Richmond, hereafter referred to as the *Goodwood Manuscripts*, is preserved in West Sussex Record Office, where three volumes deal with smuggling during the 1740s. The Duke is also thought to have been 'A Gentleman of Chichester' who wrote an account of the trial which convicted the murderers of Galley and Chater. Important documents found among the papers of Lord Shelburne (briefly Prime Minister in 1782) are referred to as the *Shelburne Documents*. These were edited and published in New York in 1928 by A L Cross as *Documents relating to the Royal Forests, the Sheriff and Smuggling*. The Customs & Excise Library has transcripts of much of the surviving correspondence between the Board of Customs and officials at the main ports (the originals are in the Public Record Office). Unfortunately, while these *Outport Letters* for Southampton and Portsmouth are good, those for Dover and the Sussex ports are meagre or non-existant. This library also preserves the *Parry Collection* of documents assembled by Sir Sydney Parry, when Deputy Chairman of the Board, from 1904 to 1925. The *Sussex Weekly Advertiser*, published at Lewes from 1749, provides the best newspaper record, but is disappointingly reticent in the early years.

The various contemporary and other sources used in each chapter are separately listed below:

Chapter 1
Contemporary Sources
'A Gentleman of Chichester' *A Full & Genuine History of the Inhuman and Unparalleled Murders of Mr William Galley. . . . And Mr Daniel Chater.* First published 1749
Parry Collection

Sayer Manuscripts
Shelburne Documents
Other Sources
Cole, W A 'Trends in eighteenth century smuggling' *Econ Hist Rev* X 1958 pp 121–143
Fraser, Duncan *The Smugglers* Montrose, 1978
Morley, Geoffrey *Smuggling in Hampshire and Dorset 1700–1850* Newbury 1983
Nichols, F F *Honest Thieves. The Violent Heyday of English Smuggling* 1973
Shore, Henry N *Smuggling Days & Smuggling Ways* 1892
Smith, Graham *Something to Declare* 1980
Teignmouth, Lord (H N Shore) & Harper, Charles G *The Smugglers* 1st pub 1923
Williams, Neville *Contraband Cargoes* 1959
Winslow, Cal 'Sussex Smugglers' in Hay, Douglas (ed) *Albion's Fatal Tree* pp 119–166 1975

Chapter 2
Contemporary Sources
Goodwood manuscripts
Parry Collection
Sayer Manuscripts
Other Sources
Bullen, Mark *The Sussex Coast Blockade for the Prevention of Smuggling, 1817–1831* Unpublished thesis 1983, in Customs & Excise library.
Chatterton, E Keble *King's Cutters & Smugglers 1700–1855* 1912
Cooper, William Durrant 'Smuggling in Sussex' *Sx Arch Coll* X 1858 pp 69–94
English's Recollections of Old Folkestone Smugglers and Smuggling Days by an Old Folkestoner Folkestone, 2nd ed 1888
Muskett, Paul 'Military operations against smuggling in Kent & Sussex 1698–1750' *J of Soc for Army Hist Research* L11 1974 pp 89–110
Phillipson, David *Smuggling: a History 1700–1970* Newton Abbott, 1973
Smith, Graham *King's Cutters. The Revenue Service & the War against Smuggling* 1983

Chapter 3
Contemporary Sources
Goodwood Manuscripts
Sayer Manuscripts
Shelburne Documents
Other Sources
Cooper, William Durrant 'Smuggling in Sussex' *Sx Arch Coll* X 1858 69-94

Martin, Frank *Rogue's River* Hornchurch, 1983
Terry, John *The Reminiscences of an Old City 'Free Trader'* 1888 (in Kent County Library)
Williams, Neville *Contraband Cargoes* 1959
Winslow, Cal 'Sussex Smugglers' in Hay, Douglas (ed) *Albion's Fatal Tree* 1975, pp 119–166

Chapter 4
Contemporary Sources
Sayer Manuscripts
Other Sources
Finn, P *The Kent Coast Blockade* Ramsgate, 1971
Harvey, Wallace *Whitstable and the French Prisoners of War* Whitstable, 3rd impression 1983
Harvey, Wallace *The Seasalter Company – A Smuggling Fraternity (1740–1854)* Whitstable, 1983
Herne Bay Press, Articles by H E Gough and C H Ilott in the newpaper collection at Herne Bay public library
Hufton, G & Baird, E *Scarecrows Legion. Smuggling in Kent & Sussex* Rochester, 1983
Lapthorne, W H *Smugglers' Broadstairs* Ramsgate, undated
Mirams, M D 'Pegwell Village' *Bygone Kent* 1982 pp 655–60
Muskett, Paul 'Edward Roots, Mariner of Rochester' *Bygone Kent* 1980 pp 71–74

Chapter 5
Contemporary Sources
Dover Outport Letters
Sayer Manuscripts
Other Sources
Banks, John *Reminiscences of Smugglers and Smuggling* 1871, repub 1966
Brent, Colin E *Smuggling through Sussex* East Sussex C.C. revised ed 1977
Brentall, Margaret *The Cinque Ports & Romney Marsh* enlarged ed 1980
Clark, Kenneth M *Smuggling in Rye and District* Rye, 1977
Cozens, L W *Smugglers of Deal v Customs* Deal, 1984
Douch, John *Smuggling. The Wicked Trade* Dover, 1980
English's Reminiscences of Old Folkestone Smugglers and Smuggling Days by an Old Folkestoner 2nd ed Folkestone, 1888
Honey W H *Smuggling in Deal* Deal Maritime Museum Leaflet, 1976
Laigle, Dominique Odile *Smuggling in Kent* Univ of Caen thesis, 1972 (in Kent County Library)
Muskett, Paul 'Gabriel Tomkins, Smuggler, Customs Officer, Sheriff's Bailiff and Highwayman' *Sussex History* 2 pp 8–17 and 3 pp 19–27

Shore, Henry N *The True History of the Aldington Smugglers* (articles in Kentish Express 1902–3, in Folkestone library)

Vidler, Leopold A *A New History of Rye* Hove, 1934

Chapter 6
Contemporary Sources
Sayer Manuscripts
Sussex Weekly Advertiser
Other Sources
Banks, John *Reminiscences of Smugglers & Smuggling* 1871 repub 1966
Bexhill-on-Sea Observer of 4th Oct 1969
Cooper, William Durrant 'Smuggling in Sussex' *Sx Arch Coll* X 1858, 69–94
Cousins, Henry *Hastings of bygone days and the present* Hastings, 1911
Crake, W V 'The Correspondence of John Collier' *Sx Arch Coll* 1902, 62–109
Kent, Philip 'Stories of a Hastings Smuggler' *Sx Co Mag* 4 1930 pp 421–2
Robertson, Charles A *Hailsham & Its Environs* 1982

Chapter 7
Contemporary Sources
Sussex Weekly Advertiser
Other Sources
Blyth, Henry *Smugglers' Village. The Story of Rottingdean* Brighton undated
Bullen, Mark *Ill Gotten Gains. The Romance and Tragedy of Sussex Smuggling 1700–1850* Unpublished thesis 1978, in Customs & Excise Library.
Bullen, Mark *The Sussex Coast Blockade for the Prevention of Smuggling 1817–1831* Unpublished research 1983, in Customs & Excise Library
Cooper, W D 'Smuggling in Sussex' *Sx Arch Coll* X 1858 pp 69–94
Doff, Elizabeth 'Celebrating a Royal Occasion in East Dean' *Sussex Genealogist* 3 1981 pp 4–11
McCarthy, E & M *Sussex River. Seaford to Newhaven* Seaford 1975
McCarthy, E & M *Five and Twenty Ponies* Alfriston 1982
Muskett, Paul 'Military Operations against Smuggling in Kent & Sussex 1698–1750' *J of Soc for Army Historical Research* LII 1974 pp 89–110
Pagden, Florence *History of Alfriston* Hove, undated
Parry, J D *An Historical and Descriptive Account of the Coast of Sussex* 1st Edn 1833, reissued 1970
Piper, A C *Afriston. The Story of a Downland Village* 1970
Richards, Bertram F 'Smuggling in Sussex 100 years ago' *Sussex County Magazine* 4 1930
Robertson, Charles A *Hailsham & its Environs* 1982

Smart, P M H *Jevington Through the Ages* Jevington 1970
The Times 'A Sussex Smuggler' April 25th 1958

Chapter 8
Contemporary Sources
Goodwood Manuscripts
Shelburne Documents
Brighton Gazette
Brighton & Hove Herald
Sussex Weekly Advertiser
Other Sources
Albery, William 'Sussex Smugglers and Smuggling' *Sx Co Mag* 8 1934
Blackman, Janet *Sussex Smugglers* Unpublished thesis in West Sussex Record Office
Cheal, Henry *The Ships and Mariners of Shoreham* 1909, repub 1981
Cheal, Henry *The Story of Shoreham* 1921, repub 1971
Evans, John *Picture of Worthing* 1805
Farrant, Sue *Georgian Brighton 1740–1820* Brighton 1980
Fleet, Charles *Glimpses of our Ancestors in Sussex* Vol I, Lewes 1878
Kerridge, R G P *A History of Lancing* 1979
Middleton, Judy *A History of Hove* 1979
Musgrave, Clifford *Life in Brighton* Chatham, 1981
Smail, Henfrey *The Worthing Road and its Coaches* Worthing, 1943
Smith, Horace et al. *Worthing Parade Two* Worthing 1954
Warter, Rev J W *The Sea-Board and the Down* Vol I 1860

Chapter 9
Contemporary Sources
'A Gentleman of Chichester' *A Full & Genuine History of the Inhuman and Unparalleled Murders of Mr William Galley . . . and Mr Daniel Chater* First published 1749
Goodwood Manuscripts
Outport Letters for the ports of Cowes, Southampton and Portsmouth
Other Sources
Arnold-Foster, D *At War with the Smugglers*, 1936
Bishop, Rev John 'The Strange Case of Thomas Lillywhite – was he a Smuggler?' *Sussex Family Historian* 4 1981 pp 282–6
Cooper, W D 'Smuggling in Sussex' *Sussex Arch Coll* X 1858 pp 69–94
Heron-Allen, Edward *Selsey Bill, Historic and Prehistoric* 1911
Hicks, John and Bulford, Michael *Contraband* Hants County Library booklet
Kent, John *Records and Reminiscences of Goodwood and the Dukes of Richmond* 1896

Lennox, C G H (Earl of March) *A Duke and his Friends* Vol II 1011
Morley, Geoffrey *Smuggling in Hampshire and Dorset 1700–1850* Newbury 1983
Nicholls, F F *Honest Thieves: the violent heyday of English Smuggling* 1973
Robinson, Joseph *Reminiscences 1820–1917* (hand-written notes by his son, in West Sussex Record Office).

Index

171

INDEX

173

Acknowledgements

Among the large number of people who have helped me in writing this book, I wish particularly to thank:

The members of staff at the Customs & Excise library, the Kent, East Sussex and West Sussex Record Offices, the Sussex Archaeological Society library and the Towner Art Gallery in Eastbourne.
Rev John Bishop
Mark Bullen
Kenneth M Clark
R J Coe
John Douch
H E Gough
Wallach Harvey
Alan Hay
W H Lapthorne
Charles A Robertson
Graham Smith